Classifying Applicants for Fair Lending Analyses:
What Do the Data Have to Say?

Jason Dietrich

August 2009

OCC Economics Working Paper 2009-4

Classifying Applicants for Fair Lending Analyses:
What Do the Data Have to Say?

Jason Dietrich
Office of the Comptroller of the Currency

August 2009

Abstract: Testing for discrimination in mortgage lending requires classifying consumers into treatment groups and control groups. Although this may seem like a straightforward task, it is actually quite complicated. Home Mortgage Disclosure Act (HMDA) data, the primary source of data for these analyses, contain information on the ethnicity, race, and gender for both primary and coapplicants. In addition, applicants have the option of reporting up to five races. Using these detailed data to construct the standard groups, such as "Black," "Hispanic," and "White," requires subjective decisions on how to appropriately aggregate applications.

This study uses a data-driven approach to classify applications, minimizing subjectivity. Using HMDA data, as well as data from a recent examination conducted by the Office of the Comptroller of the Currency, we disaggregated applications into the most basic subsets the HMDA data allowed. Our objectives are to better understand the characteristics of applicants, analyze variation in denial rates across underlying subsets of applications, and develop a data-driven classification strategy that could be used during fair lending analyses.

Keywords: Protected Class, Discrimination, Fair Lending

Jason Dietrich is an Economist in the Compliance Risk Analysis Division at the Office of the Comptroller of the Currency. Please address correspondence to Jason Dietrich, Economist, Compliance Risk Analysis Division, Office of the Comptroller of the Currency, 250 E Street SW, Washington, DC 20219 (phone: 202-874-5119; e-mail: jason.dietrich@occ.treas.gov).

The views expressed in this paper are those of the author alone and do not necessarily reflect those of the Office of the Comptroller of the Currency or the U.S. Department of the Treasury. The author would like to thank John Karikari, Ioan Voicu, Gary Whalen, Lily Chin, and Famin Ahmed for their insightful comments and editorial assistance.

I. Introduction

Recent changes in how ethnicity and race are reported under HMDA have generated much discussion on the appropriate definitions of treatment groups and control groups for fair lending analyses. HMDA data contain information on ethnicity, race, and gender for the primary applicant and any coapplicants.In addition, applicants can report belonging to up to five racial groups (classifications are listed in table 1). Although such detailed data are typically useful for analyses, such detail can make it difficult to classify applicants into groups. The most difficult applications to classify are joint applications, in which the primary and coapplicants report different ethnicities, races, or genders, and any applications in which individual applicants have reported more than one race. Currently, different regulators use different classification strategies. This has created challenges for lenders, especially those with multiple subsidiaries that report to more than one regulator. This begs the question of whether there is one, appropriate definition of treatment groups and control groups that regulators and researchers should use.[1] The Equal Credit Opportunity Act lists the various factors lenders cannot consider during credit transactions but offers no guidance on how to actually classify applicants for analyses. Therefore, classification is left to regulators' discretion and requires some subjective judgment.

This study minimizes the subjectivity in the classification process by letting the data identify subsets of applicants that can be combined. Specifically, we allow the data

---

[1] There is extensive literature on strategies for classifying individuals for analyses. For a sample of recent works, see Bell (1996), Campbell (2007), Aspinall (1997), James (2001), Robbin (1999), Holloway and Wyly (2002), Williams (1999), Huck (2001), Hirschman *et al* (2000), and Saperstein (2006). Full references are listed at the end of the article.

to convey the classification strategy based on similarities in denial rates for the most disaggregate ethnic, racial, and gender groups possible with the given HMDA data. Using 2005 HMDA data, we first identify the ethnic, racial, and gender groups to which each application could possibly belong. Each of these aggregate groups is partitioned into mutually exclusive subsets or base units based on the specific values of the HMDA ethnic, racial, and gender variables. We analyzed the distribution of applications and variation in denial rates across subsets. After this initial analysis of raw HMDA data, we used data from a fair lending examination the Office of the Comptroller of the Currency (OCC) recently conducted to analyze the same relationships after accounting for differences in creditworthiness.

This study has three objectives. First, we develop a clearer understanding of the types of applicants that comprise the aggregate ethnic, racial, and gender groups typically used for fair lending analyses. Second, we assess the level of variation in denial rates across underlying subsets of the aggregate groupings. Little variation suggests aggregation is at appropriate levels. Large variation suggests applicants in the subsets are either different in some systematic way or are treated differently in some systematic way. Regardless, such results suggest aggregate groups are inappropriate and subsets should be analyzed separately. Finally, we develop a data-driven classification strategy that can be used during fair lending analyses.

The remainder of the paper is constructed as follows. Section II details the empirical approach used throughout this study. Section III characterizes the applicants that comprise the aggregate ethnic, racial, and gender groups typically used during fair lending analyses. Section IV analyzes variation in denial rates for the disaggregate subsets comprising the aggregate groups. Section V summarizes how the data-driven approach would be used during a full fair lending analysis. Section VI concludes the discussion.

II. Summary of Data-Driven Approach

This section outlines the basic components of the data-driven approach used in this study. The base dataset we used, and that is used for most fair lending analyses, is HMDA data. HMDA requires lenders to gather and report data on the ethnicity, race, and gender of primary applicants and coapplicants. Table 1 lists all possible values for these variables.[2,3] The "No coapplicant" option is only relevant for coapplicant variables, so each coapplicant variable has one more possible value than its corresponding primary applicant variable. In addition, each applicant has the option of reporting up to five races. Therefore, whereas ethnicity and gender only have one primary applicant variable and one coapplicant variable, for race, there are five primary applicant variables and five coapplicant variables.

Using these data, we begin the analysis by constructing nine aggregate groups: two ethnicities (Hispanic and non-Hispanic); five races (American Indian, Asian, Black, Native Hawaiian, and White); and two genders (female and male). If a primary applicant or coapplicant reports belonging to a given group, that application is classified into that group. The purpose of this initial classification is to identify all applications that could

---

[2] See *A Guide to HMDA Reporting: Getting it Right!* (March 2009) for details on HMDA reporting requirements.

[3] With Statistical Policy Directive 15, the Office of Management and Budget (OMB) set guidelines to provide consistent racial and ethnic classifications across government agencies. Revisions to this directive, which was implemented in 1997, formed the 2004 revised guidelines on how race and ethnicity data would be gathered and reported. The 2004 revisions considered the capability of either disaggregating or collapsing groups of individuals depending on the frequency of reported combinations. This is the approach we took in this study. For more details, see *OMB Revisions to the Standards for the Classification of Federal Data on Race and Ethnicity.*

potentially be coded into a particular aggregate group given the available variables in

HMDA. Applications reporting no specific ethnicity, race, or gender are excluded from

the analysis.

Table 1: HMDA Ethnicity, Race, and Gender Codes		
Ethnicity	**Race**	**Gender**
1: Hispanic or Latino	1: American Indian or Alaska Native	1: Male
2: Not Hispanic or Latino	2: Asian	2: Female
3: Information not provided by applicant in mail, Internet, or telephone application	3: Black or African American	3: Information not provided by applicant in mail, Internet, or telephone application
4: Not applicable	4: Native Hawaiian or other Pacific Islander	4: Not applicable
5: No coapplicant	5: White	5: No coapplicant
	6: Information not provided by applicant in mail, Internet, or telephone application	
	7: Not applicable	
	8: No coapplicant	

Once this original aggregate classification is complete, we construct all possible

underlying subsets of these aggregate groups. These underlying subsets are defined by

the combinations of values reported for the primary applicant and coapplicant. We take a

purely data-driven approach in this study, so the reporting order matters. Therefore, for

ethnicity, because there are four possible values for the primary applicant and five

possible values for the coapplicant, there are 20 ($n = 4 \times 5$) possible underlying subsets.

Eight of these subsets contain "Hispanic" and, therefore, would fall under the aggregate

Hispanic group. Similarly, eight contain "non-Hispanic" and would fall under the

aggregate non-Hispanic group. The structure of the ethnicity and gender variables is

similar, so there are 20 gender subsets in all; eight female and eight male. Race is considerably complicated, because both the primary applicant and coapplicant can report up to five races. For a given race, there are 261 possible unique combinations of the five HMDA race variables that include that race.[4] Because these 261 combinations are also possible for coapplicants, there are 68,121 (n = 261 × 261) possible combinations for joint applications. Adding in the 261 possible combinations for single applicants yields 68,382 possible underlying subsets for a given race. Although this is a large number, as we show throughout this article, the number of subsets with data is actually small and manageable.

To make the presentation and discussion of these subsets more manageable, we use combinations of values for the primary and coapplicant HMDA variables instead of specific descriptions. For example, instead of saying, "the subset consists of a primary applicant who is Hispanic and a coapplicant who is non-Hispanic," we simply use the subset code 12. This is especially useful for the discussion of racial subsets, because these subsets are defined by combinations of 10 values. For example, the subset, "primary applicant reported both Black and Asian, and the coapplicant reported Black," would be presented as 3200030000. As an example of these subsets and the coding used to discuss the results, table 2 shows the eight possible underlying subsets of the aggregate Hispanic group, along with the subset code.

---

[4] We are assuming no instances in which race1 is a missing value and race2 is a non-missing value. Also, we do not include values of race representing "mail, Internet, telephone" or "NA." Finally, we deem placement of information as important, so a combination such as race1 = Black, race2 = Asian is treated differently than race1 = Asian, race2 = Black.

Table 2: All Possible Underlying Subsets for Aggregate Hispanic Group		
Primary Applicant	**Coapplicant**	**Subset Code**
Hispanic	Hispanic	11
Hispanic	Non-Hispanic	12
Hispanic	Mail, telephone, Internet	13
Hispanic	Not applicable	14
Hispanic	No coapplicant	15
Non-Hispanic	Hispanic	21
Mail, telephone, Internet	Hispanic	31
Not applicable	Hispanic	41

Within this structure, the actual analysis consists of two parts. The first part uses HMDA data from 2005 and focuses on raw disparities and signals of fair lending risk. Following banking regulators' strategy of conducting bank-specific fair lending exams, we conduct this analysis at the bank level. Because disaggregation creates sample size issues, we only include the 22 largest national banks as of 2005.[5] Throughout this analysis of HMDA data, we focus on applications for first lien, owner-occupied, inhabited by one-to-four families (1-4 family), conventional home purchase loans.

Table 3 shows the comparisons we make in the analysis of HMDA data. The table presents results for one lender and one aggregate group—Hispanics. For this lender, 37.1 percent of the aggregate Hispanic group was denied credit. As we noted, the aggregate Hispanic group can be partitioned into eight underlying subsets. Table 3 presents the denial rates for each of these eight subsets. As the table shows, only five of these subsets had applications. Of these five subsets, the variation in denial rates was quite high, ranging from 21.3 percent to 39.4 percent. Interestingly, based on the denial rates, the five subsets can be combined into two distinct groups. Single applicants and joint

---

[5] We chose to focus on the 22 largest national banks, because statistical analyses are most accurate when applied to large volumes of applications, and these are the institutions where statistical modeling is most commonly used during fair lending analyses. These 22 national banks may not be representative of all HMDA reporters.

applications in which both applicants are Hispanic, both have denial rates near 39
percent. The remaining three subsets all have denial rates near 22 percent. These patterns
strongly indicate which subsets could possibly be combined.

With the analysis of HMDA data, we address the following two questions. First,
what is the composition of the aggregate groups? Specifically, for each of the nine
aggregate groups, what percentage comes from each of the underlying subsets? Second,
what do the denial rates for the underlying subsets look like? Is the variation across
subsets high or low? Significant variation suggests applicants in the subsets are
systematically different in some way or are receiving systematically different treatment.
Regardless, such results suggest that the subsets should be analyzed separately and not
aggregated.

The second part of the analysis uses data from a fair lending examination the OCC
recently conducted. This analysis focuses on denial rate disparities after first accounting
for applicant and product characteristics. The populations analyzed and models estimated
are the same as those used during the actual examination. The objective is to provide an
example of how to apply a data-driven approach to fair lending analyses.

Table 3: Variation in Denial Rates for Underlying Groups Comprising Hispanic Applicants for Lender 1
Denial Rate for Aggregate Hispanic Group, n = 37.1%

Primary Applicant	Coapplicant	Number	Denial Rate
Hispanic	Hispanic	15,111	38.4%
Hispanic	Non-Hispanic	2,483	22.4%
Hispanic	Mail, telephone, Internet application	81	22.2%
Hispanic	Not applicable	0	–
Hispanic	No coapplicant	26,546	39.4%
Non-Hispanic	Hispanic	2,723	21.3%
Mail, telephone, Internet application	Hispanic	0	–
Not applicable	Hispanic	0	–

III. Who Are These People?

The first objective of this study is to develop a better understanding of the applicants who could be classified into each of the nine aggregate groups. Disaggregating the data into all possible subsets for each aggregate group at the lender level generates a large volume of output, so we summarize the results in tables 4 and 5. Appendix A contains the full set of results of numbers of applications and denial rates by lender for each aggregate group.[6]

Table 4 summarizes the composition of the five aggregate racial groups across lenders. We identify the underlying subsets that typically had the highest and second highest numbers of applications (as explained in the Table 4 footnotes). These results are based on subsets with at least 30 applications. Not surprisingly, for all four racial minorities, single applicants always comprise the largest subset, whereas joint applications in which both applicants were the same race always comprise the second largest subset. For White applicants, these two subsets make up the two largest groups, but single applicants comprise the largest subset for only about half of the lenders.

---

[6] The tables in appendix A contain only information on subsets with at least 30 applications.

Table 4: Summary of Composition of Aggregate Racial Groups
(Mean and Range Across Lenders of Percent of Applications From Stated Subset)

	American Indian* (N = 12 lenders)		Asian‡ (N = 19 lenders)		Black§ (N = 19 lenders)		Native Hawaiian** (N = 11 lenders)		White‡‡ (N = 21 lenders)	
	Mean (%)	Min, Max (%)	Mean (%)	Min, Max (%)	Mean (%)	Min, Max (%)	Mean (%)	Min, Max (%)	Mean (%)	Min, Max (%)
Single applicants	45.8	31.5, 62.7	51.2	36.3, 73.2	71.3	38.8, 89.5	43.9	19.2, 53.3	49.9	30.8, 69.6
Joint applicants with same race (no multiple races)	20.7	7.9, 39.2	33.2	20.7, 43.0	20.0	8.9, 28.7	20.8	5.8, 29.9	47.4	27.0, 66.2
Applications containing specific race and White (joint or multiple)	25.5	7.1, 44.7	13.1	4.3, 24.2	6.1	0, 20.4	25.0	2.6, 65.4	NA	NA
Applications containing specific race and another minority (joint or multiple)	4.8	0.6, 11.1	1.1	0.0, 3.4	1.4	0.0, 10.2	6.1	3.4, 9.4	NA	NA
Applications containing specific race, White, and another minority (joint or multiple)	1.9	0.0, 3.7	0.3	0.0, 1.0	0.3	0, 2.0	1.9	0, 5.8	NA	NA
Applications containing specific race and some race other than White or another minority (joint or multiple)	1.3	0.0, 4.2	1.2	0.0, 3.0	1.0	0, 4.1	2.3	0.0, 14.3	NA	NA

* Largest subset was single (i.e., individual) applicants for all lenders; second largest subset was joint American Indian applications for all lenders.
‡ Largest subset was single applicants for all lenders; second largest was joint Asian applications for all lenders.
§ Largest subset was single applicants for all lenders; second largest was joint Black applications for all lenders.
** Largest subset was single applicants for all lenders; second largest was joint Native Hawaiian applications for all lenders. For 11 of 20 lenders, single applicants comprised the largest subset and joint white applications comprised the second largest; for 10 of 21 lenders, joint white applications comprised the largest subset and single, white applications comprised the second largest. One lender did not have at least 30 applications for single, White applicants.
‡‡ Largest and second largest subsets of applications varied by lender. For 11 of 20 lenders, single applicants comprised the largest subset and joint white applications comprised the second largest; for 10 of 21 lenders, joint white applications comprised the largest subset and single, white applications comprised the second largest. One lender did not have at least 30 applications for single, White applicants.

11

Table 4 presents summary statistics for composition percentages across lenders. For each aggregate racial group, there are 68,382 possible underlying subsets. It is difficult to clearly convey results for all of these subsets, so we compress these base subsets into six more aggregate subsets: (1) single applicants; (2) joint applications with same race (no multiple race applicants); (3) single (multiple race) or joint applications containing only the specific race and White applicants; (4) single (multiple race) or joint applications containing only the specific race and one or more other minorities; (5) single (multiple race) or joint applications containing the specific race, White applicants, and one or more other minorities; and (6) single (multiple race) or joint applications containing the specific race and some race other than White and another minority. For each race, we computed the percent of total applications in each of these more aggregate subsets. These calculations were done separately for each lender. Summary statistics of these percentages are then constructed across lenders with at least 30 home purchase applications.

For an example of how to read table 4, look at the two columns for American Indians. In the 2005 HMDA data, 12 of 22 lenders analyzed in this study reported at least 30 home purchase applications that could be categorized into the aggregate American Indian group.[7] For each of these 12 lenders, we calculated the percent of American Indian applications that fell into each of the six more aggregate subsets mentioned in table 4. Table 4 shows that, on average, single applicants comprise 45.8 percent of the

---

[7] Table A1a in appendix A shows results for American Indians for only 10 lenders. In that table, results for a lender are included only if at least one of the base subsets has at least 30 applications. The 30 application requirement is applied to each subset, because denial rates are calculated for each subset. Here, results for a lender are included if the aggregate group has at least 30 applications. The 30-application requirement is applied at the aggregate level here, because we are calculating percentages of the total aggregate group, i.e., the denominator for these percentages is the total number of applications in the aggregate group.

aggregate American Indian group. The range for these percentages across the 12 lenders is 31.5 to 62.7 percent.

Table 4 highlights a number of interesting results. First, not surprisingly, single applicants comprise the largest portion of the aggregate racial groups, on average. The average percentages are all fairly similar, except for that of Black applicants, which is approximately 25 percentage points higher. Second, for each race except American Indians and Native Hawaiians, joint applications with the same race is the second largest contributor on average. For American Indians and Native Hawaiians, the second largest contributor is applications including both the minority applicant and a White applicant. These results differ slightly from those presented in the first two rows because of different sample size criteria (i.e., 30 applications per subset versus 30 total applications), as well as the aggregation we use for the bottom portion of the table. Third, on average, the contribution of mixed applicants is generally small. The largest average percentage is for applications from a Native Hawaiian and another minority at 6.1 percent. There are, however, specific instances where the contribution of these groups is fairly large. For example, at one lender, applications from an American Indian and another minority comprise 11.1 percent of American Indian applications. Finally, White applications comprise almost solely single applicant Whites or joint applications in which both applicants are White. For every lender, these two subsets combine for at least 93 percent of total applications in the aggregate White group.

Table 5 presents corresponding results for ethnicity and gender. Because of the smaller numbers of possible subsets, the only aggregation we apply here is to group joint applications where ethnicity or gender is provided for one applicant, but "Mail, telephone, Internet" or "NA" (not applicable) is provided for the other applicant. For the most part, the ethnicity results are similar to the racial results. Single applicants comprise the largest portion and joint applications in which both applicants report the same ethnicity is next largest. One difference between the ethnic and racial results is the volume of mixed applications, especially for Hispanics. On average, 7.4 percent of Hispanic applications have a Hispanic primary applicant and non-Hispanic coapplicant, with a range of 1.5 to 15.3 percent. In addition, a mean 8.0 percent of Hispanic applications have a non-Hispanic primary applicant and a Hispanic coapplicant, with a range of 0 to 19.9 percent. These larger percentages are not seen for non-Hispanics, because non-Hispanics are a much larger group on average (i.e., the denominators in the percentages are larger).

The gender results are somewhat different. Not surprisingly, the largest contributor to both the aggregate female and male groups is joint applications in which the primary applicant is male and the coapplicant is female. A mean of more than 50 percent of applications come from this subset, with ranges from 37.3 to 81.2 percent for females and 33.0 to 70.5 percent for males. The second largest subset on average for both females and males consists of single applicants. Joint applications in which the primary applicant is female and the coapplicant is male also show a fairly high contribution. For both the aggregate female and male groups, the mean contribution from this subset is around 8.5 percent with a range of 4 to 15 percent. In general, the other two subsets have small contributions.

Table 5: Summary of Composition of Aggregate Ethnic and Gender Groups
(Mean and Range Across Lenders of Percent of Applications From Stated Subset)

Subset Description	Hispanic* (N = 19 lenders)		Non-Hispanic‡ (N = 21 lenders)		Subset Description	Female§ (N = 21 lenders)		Male** (N = 21 lenders)	
	Mean (%)	Min, Max	Mean (%)	Min, Max		Mean (%)	Min, Max	Mean (%)	Min, Max
Single applicant	55.3	33.6, 74.5	51.7	30.0, 69.9	Single applicant	33.2	13.9, 51.4	39.5	23.9, 60.3
Joint application with same ethnicity	28.1	19.4, 50.5	45.8	27.3, 67.2	Joint application with same gender	1.3	0, 2.1	1.5	0, 3.1
Hispanic/non-Hispanic	7.4	1.5, 15.3	0.7	0, 1.3	Female/male	8.9	4.3, 15.3	8.0	3.7, 14.5
Non-Hispanic/Hispanic	8.0	0, 19.9	0.9	0, 2.2	Male/female	56.2	37.3, 81.2	50.4	33.0, 70.5
Group and something else	1.2	0, 5.3	0.9	0.2, 5.6	Group and something else	0.4	0, 1.9	0.6	0, 3.2

* Largest subset: single applicants (18 of 19 lenders). Second largest subset: joint Hispanic applications (17 of 18 lenders). One lender did not have at least 30 applications in which both applicants were Hispanic. This type of issue occurred for both the female and male results as well.
‡ Largest subset: single applicants (13 of 20 lenders); joint non-Hispanic applications (7 of 20 lenders). Second largest subset: joint non-Hispanic applications (13 of 20 lenders); single applicants (7 of 20 lenders).
§ Largest subset: male/female joint applications (19 of 21 lenders). Second largest subset: single applicants (18 of 20 lenders).
** Largest subset: male/female joint applications (16 of 21 lenders). Second largest subset: single applicants (15 of 20 lenders).

15

The purpose of this section is to gain a better understanding of the applications that could be classified into each of the aggregate ethnic, racial, and gender groups. Overall, for ethnicity and race, single applicants and joint applications of similar ethnicity and race comprise the majority of applications. This is fortunate, because there is little question about how to classify these applications. There are, however, many examples for which mixed ethnic or racial applications are a significant contributor to the aggregate groups. This creates challenges for analyses, because these applications are difficult to classify. The issues with gender classifications are slightly different, because mixed joint applications with a male and female are so common. As a result, classifying applicants into aggregate gender groups is generally more difficult.

IV. Denial Rates

This section analyzes variation in denial rates across the underlying subsets of each of the nine aggregate groups. High variation suggests that the underlying subsets are systematically different or receiving systematically different treatment. In such instances, these subsets should be analyzed separately, instead of being combined. Low variation suggests aggregation is appropriate.

As a first step in this analysis, we construct denial rates for each of the aggregate groups, as well as each underlying subset with at least 30 applications. For each lender, this yields a total of nine aggregate denial rates, with denial rates for up to eight subsets for ethnicity and gender, and up to 68,382 subsets for race. For each lender, we compute the difference between the denial rate for each subset and the denial rate for its corresponding aggregate group. For example, for each lender, we construct the denial rate for Hispanics. In addition, for each lender, we also construct denial rates for each of the eight mutually exclusive subsets comprising the aggregate Hispanic group. For each of these subset denial rates, we subtract the overall denial rate for Hispanics. We then analyze the variation in these differences.

Table 6 presents results for the analysis of racial subsets and table 7 presents results for the analyses of ethnic and gender subsets. Each table presents the number of subsets that have 30 or more applications, the denial rate for the aggregate group, and the minimum and maximum values of differences between denial rates for underlying subsets and their corresponding aggregate groups. To interpret the tables, look at the first row for Black applicants. Results are for lender 1. For this lender, the aggregate denial rate is 37.5 percent. There are 11 subsets of the aggregate Black group with at least 30 applications. The specific subsets can be found in table A3a in Appendix A. One of these subsets has a denial rate of 27.7 percent, which is 9.8 percentage points lower than the aggregate denial rate. The highest denial rate among the subsets is 58.0 percent, which is 20.5 percentage points higher than the aggregate denial rate.

Interpret the minimum (min) and maximum (max) values in tables 6 and 7 with care, because their values are affected by the aggregate denial rate. Extremely high and low aggregate denial rates restrict the magnitude of deviations from this denial rate. Specifically, high aggregate denial rates limit the possible max values and low aggregate denial rates limit the possible min values. Consequently, the min values tend to be lower for such groups as White applicants and Asians who generally have lower aggregate denial rates. Black applicants and Hispanics, who generally have higher aggregate denial rates, tend to have higher min values. As a result, the min and max values should

Table 6: Deviations Between Denial Rates for Aggregate Groups and Denial Rates of Underlying Subsets: Race

Lender	American Indian				Asian				Black				Native Hawaiian				White			
	N	Agg. Rate	Min	Max	N	Agg. Rate	Min	Max	N	Agg. Rate	Min	Max	N	Agg. Rate	Min	Max	N	Agg. Rate	Min	Max
1	10	39.1	-12.9	18.9	15	20.2	-8.3	18.0	11	37.5	-9.8	20.5	7	35.1	-19.9	6.9	25	19.8	-18.0	20.3
2*																				
3					2	3.7	-1.8	2.4	2	11.5	-3.9	1.4					2	3.1	-0.8	1.0
4					1	2.0	1.9	1.9	1	10.9	0.1	0.1					2	14.1	-0.7	1.5
5	2	17.9	-8.9	4.1	4	6.9	-3.7	2.9	2	22.4	-10.1	3.2	1	18.2	9.6	9.6	4	7.0	-2.8	2.9
6					2	6.9	-1.3	2.6									2	23.2	-10.0	10.3
7									2	17.0	0.1	0.9					7	6.2	-1.8	1.8
8	1	8.3	1.0	1.0	4	5.6	-1.9	4.5	3	14.6	-5.3	1.7	1	8.9	6.6	6.6	6	5.1	-1.4	5.1
9					2	7.6	-2.2	1.7	3	20.2	-7.2	6.5					5	8.9	-8.9	17.8
10	4	17.7	-8.1	1.0	5	15.8	-2.5	0.9	5	23.9	-12.0	1.1	4	20.5	-1.5	2.5	14	13.7	-4.1	9.3
11									2	30.4	-7.5	1.4					2	21.6	-3.6	2.9
12																	1	3.2	-0.2	-0.2
13	8	17.8	-5.9	2.8	9	14.0	-7.3	4.4	8	19.0	-7.2	4.4	7	14.5	-8.7	4.4	21	11.8	-6.0	8.8
14									1	23.4	0.0	0.0					2	23.3	-4.2	5.3
15					2	8.9	-2.2	3.3	1	13.5	1.2	1.2					2	12.7	-1.9	2.2
16	1	36.8	7.0	7.0	4	17.1	-12.0	3.4	4	46.9	-13.5	1.8	2	27.5	-7.5	5.4	8	17.7	-12.6	24.3
17					2	11.8	0.3	3.3									2	10.4	-1.0	1.4
18	2	26.8	-2.2	3.3	4	15.3	-9.1	1.5	4	20.6	-15.3	1.1	2	20.7	-4.2	5.6	9	10.0	-10.0	1.8
19	11	16.6	-5.8	5.1	19	8.5	-8.5	14.0	10	22.4	-14.6	8.5	8	13.7	-13.7	8.8	31	8.8	-4.4	22.1
20					2	18.7	2.5	5.6									3	8.8	-1.2	5.5
21	2	6.3	-3.1	2.2	3	7.2	0.1	2.5	2	11.3	-4.4	2.3					3	7.5	-0.2	2.2
22	5	68.1	-12.0	5.3	6	51.6	-2.0	15.5	5	63.7	-8.8	6.0	4	62.9	-12.9	1.7	15	61.0	-11.0	8.7

* Lender 2 did not meet the sample size requirements for any of the racial groups for our study.
Abbreviations: Agg. rate means aggregate denial rate; min means minimum; max means maximum; N means number.

18

Table 7: Deviations Between Denial Rates for Aggregate Groups and Denial Rates of Underlying Subsets: Ethnicity and Gender

Lender	Hispanic				Non-Hispanic				Female				Male			
	N	Agg. Rate	Min	Max	N	Agg. Rate	Min	Max	N	Agg. Rate	Min	Max	N	Agg. Rate	Min	Max
1	5	37.1	−15.8	2.3	6	18.6	−3.4	3.8	7	19.8	−17.6	9.1	7	21.2	−18.6	9.9
2*																
3	4	8.2	−5.2	7.9	4	3.6	−1.5	1.6	4	3.1	−0.8	3.6	4	3.7	−3.7	2.4
4	2	22.3	−1.9	2.8	2	4.5	−2.4	1.3	3	12.7	−2.4	1.0	3	11.8	−1.5	1.9
5	4	17.6	−15.6	4.4	4	7.5	−5.5	3.5	4	6.3	−2.1	4.2	4	7.2	−3.0	5.2
6					2	27.5	−11.3	11.3	2	22.4	−7.9	17.9	2	24.4	−9.9	14.2
7	3	19.5	−8.4	3.6	3	5.2	−1.7	5.9	4	5.6	−1.8	3.1	4	6.3	−2.5	3.3
8	4	9.5	−3.5	0.7	5	5.4	−1.5	2.1	4	5.3	−1.4	2.1	5	5.4	−1.5	5.5
9	4	15.7	−4.9	3.8	4	9.5	−3.2	3.6	4	8.1	−2.3	3.8	4	8.7	−2.9	4.0
10	6	18.4	−11.5	12.3	6	13.9	−1.3	1.0	7	13.9	−4.8	3.4	7	14.3	−1.8	5.7
11	2	32.7	−5.1	9.7	2	22.8	−4.8	3.5	3	21.1	−3.9	5.3	3	21.9	−4.7	4.6
12									1	9.4	−1.5	−1.5	1	6.5	1.4	1.4
13	6	17.1	−7.6	1.4	6	12.2	−2.9	3.4	7	12.2	−2.7	10.5	7	12.7	−3.3	5.9
14	1	32.8	−0.2	−0.2	2	23.1	−3.3	6.5	3	24.2	−5.0	5.5	3	26.1	−3.0	3.7
15	2	22.2	−2.9	8.7	2	12.3	−2.5	2.5	4	11.5	−1.4	1.9	3	12.7	−2.7	4.1
16	4	37.8	−17.2	5.4	6	18.4	−5.9	23.6	6	17.3	−4.6	25.6	5	19.0	−6.3	23.3
17	2	22.9	−2.4	0.8	2	10.8	−1.5	1.2	3	10.0	−0.3	1.0	4	11.9	−2.2	14.1
18	4	18.3	−6.3	1.3	6	10.8	−4.9	2.0	5	9.7	−4.1	3.8	6	10.8	−10.8	6.4
19	6	17.1	−7.9	3.5	6	8.9	−2.3	2.4	7	8.7	−2.1	19.5	7	9.2	−2.5	6.1
20	2	10.2	−5.5	6.9	2	9.5	−1.5	3.0	3	8.3	−0.9	6.7	4	8.7	−1.4	10.0
21	4	8.1	−1.0	1.2	4	7.6	−0.5	0.4	4	7.5	−0.2	0.7	4	7.8	−1.0	0.6
22	6	65.5	−8.3	2.0	6	58.4	−2.6	9.5	6	59.3	−7.1	7.9	5	60.3	−3.8	8.7

* Lender 2 did not meet the sample size requirements for any of the ethnic or gender groups for our study.

Abbreviations: Agg. rate means aggregate denial rate; min means minimum; max means maximum; N means number.

be interpreted relative to the aggregate denial rate.[8] For example, for Hispanics for lender 3, the aggregate denial rate is only 8.2 percent. Thus, the largest min value possible is –8.2 for subsets with a denial rate of 0 percent. In this example, the minimum deviation was –5.2 percent. Although this is a relatively small number, it is actually quite large relative to the aggregate denial rate of 8.2 percent.

There are two main results in tables 6 and 7. First, clearly, there are enough underlying subsets with 30 or more applications for a statistical analysis of these subsets to be feasible at the lender level. Even for Native Hawaiians, a relatively small population, seven lenders had at least two subsets with 30 or more applications. Of course, sample size issues may be problematic for lenders with smaller volumes and for populations defined on more dimensions than what is possible with HMDA data. Second, denial rates vary considerably across underlying subsets that comprise the aggregate groups. For example, for lender 1, denial rates for the 10 American Indian subsets range from 18.9 percent above the aggregate denial rate to 12.9 percent below the aggregate denial rate. For lender 10, the denial rates for the six Hispanic subsets range from 12.3 percent above the aggregate denial rate to 11.5 percent below the aggregate denial rate. Although variation is not high in all instances, such examples are found throughout the results. The extent of this variation suggests that aggregation should not be conducted until characteristics of underlying subsets are first analyzed.

In addition to raw variation in denial rates, we searched the results in appendix A for patterns in the denial rates across subsets. A number of interesting patterns exist. First, denial rates for single applicants are almost always higher than denial rates for joint

---

[8] We contemplated presenting the range results as a percent of the aggregate denial rate. However, we felt that the difference measures were easier to understand and readers can construct percent differences if desired.

applicants of the same race and ethnicity. For lenders for which denial rates are available for both subsets, single applicants have a higher denial rate for American Indians at seven of eight lenders, for Asians at 14 of 16 lenders, for Black applicants at 13 of 14 lenders, for Native Hawaiians at six of seven lenders, for White applicants at 18 of 20 lenders, and for non-Hispanics at 19 of 20 lenders. The one exception is for Hispanics, for whom single applicants have a higher denial rate for only 10 of 18 lenders. There are no such systematic patterns for gender.

Second, for gender, there is a clear pattern in denial rates between male/female joint applications in which the male is the primary applicant and joint applications in which the female is the primary applicant. Specifically, joint applications for which the female is the primary applicant have a higher denial rate at 17 of 19 lenders. There are no such patterns for joint applications from Hispanics and non-Hispanics.

Finally, joint applications for which both applicants are male or both applicants are female generally have the highest denial rates. For the 14 lenders with at least 30 joint applications from two women, this subset has the highest denial rate for six of these lenders and is in the top two for 10 lenders. Similarly, for the 14 lenders with at least 30 joint applications from two men, this subset has the highest denial rate for seven of these lenders and is in the top two for nine lenders.

The variation in denial rates across subsets and these subset-specific patterns in denial rates suggest that these underlying subsets are systematically different in some way or receiving systematically different treatment. When such instances are identified in the data, further analysis of the underlying groups is warranted.

V. Data-Driven Approach

The final objective of this study is to develop a classification strategy that requires minimum judgment and is feasible for fair lending analyses. We have argued that a data-driven approach, through which groupings are based on patterns in the data, meets this objective. This section shows how this data-driven approach would be applied in practice, using a dataset from a fair lending examination the OCC recently conducted. The focus of this examination consists of underwriting decisions on applications for 1-4 family, owner-occupied, conventional refinance loans. The final model specification, based on the lender's policies, includes controls for FICO score, loan-to-value ratio (LTV), debt-to-income ratio (DTI), number of minor derogatories, number of major derogatories, lien status, term, assets, and applicant's self-employment status. Using this population and model specification, we use a data-driven approach to test for disparate treatment by ethnicity (Hispanics relative to non-Hispanics), race (Black applicants relative to White applicants), and gender (females relative to males). We now summarize each step of the data-driven approach.

Step 1: Identify Minority Subsets

As a first step, we identify all subsets of the minority groups Black, Hispanic, and female with at least one application in the examination dataset. Tables 8-10 list these subsets for Blacks, Hispanics, and females, respectively. These are the base minority subsets available for analysis. Subsets with at least 50 approvals and 50 denials are listed first in the column labeled, "Sufficient Number to Model." Based on the OCC's Fair

Table 8: Denial Rates for Subsets of Aggregate Racial Groups for Example Examination

Black									White Subsets With No Minorities*		
Sufficient Number to Model			Small Subsets			Very Small Subsets (sample size < 30)			Sufficient Number to Model		
Subset Code	N	Denial Rate (%)	Subset Code	N	Denial Rate (%)	Subset Code	N	Number Denied	Subset Code	N	Denial Rate (%)‡
3000080000	4,119	42.7	3500080000	45	51.1	3400080000	3	3	5000060000	1,418	33.2
3000060000	165	41.8	6000030000	41	31.7	3500040000	1	1	5000080000	33,086	32.1
3000030000	1,676	34.8	5000030000	135	28.9	3000013000	2	2	6000050000	328	29.9
3000050000	171	34.5				1300030000	1	1	5000050000	29,204	26.3
						1300050000	1	1			
						6000035000	1	1			
						2350023500	1	1			
						1300013000	1	1			
						5300080000	2	2			
						5000013000	1	1			
						1300080000	7	6			
						3000010000	4	3			
						3500035000	15	8			
						5000023000	2	1			
						1350080000	2	1			
						2300080000	2	1			
						3500013000	2	1			
						2000030000	12	6			
						4000030000	7	3			
						3500050000	5	2			
						1000030000	4	1			
						3000020000	17	4			
						3000040000	9	2			
						5000035000	10	2			
						1350050000	1	0			
						5000053000	1	0			
						3500030000	4	0			
						3450080000	1	0			
						1500013500	1	0			
						5300053000	1	0			
						3000035000	4	0			

* No small or very small subsets.

‡ Test of null hypothesis of joint equality of denial rates across subsets: $\chi^2 = 253.35$, P value = 0.00.

Table 9: Denial Rates for Subsets of Aggregate Ethnic Groups for Example Examination

Hispanic

Sufficient Number to Model			Small Subsets			Very Small Subsets (sample size <30)		
Subset Code	N	Denial Rate (%)	Subset Code	N	Denial Rate (%)	Subset Code	N	Number of Denials
15	4,980	40.9	31	39	30.8	14	1	1
13	225	40.0						
11	2,392	33.7						
12	800	26.9						
21	833	24.1						

Non-Hispanic Subsets With No Hispanics

Sufficient Number to Model			Very Small Subsets (sample size <30)		
Subset Code	N	Denial Rate (%)*	Subset Code	N	Number of Denials
23	1,476	37.2	42	1	1
25	36,716	33.4			
32	184	28.8			
22	31,049	26.8			

* Test of null hypothesis of joint equality of denial rates across subsets: $\chi^2 = 374.17$, P value = 0.00.

Table 10: Denial Rates for Subsets of Aggregate Gender Groups for Example Examination

Female

Sufficient Number to Model			Small Subsets		
Subset Code	N	Denial Rate (%)	Subset Code	N	Denial Rate (%)
23	616	39.3	32	124	37.1
25	19,110	34.8			
21	7,909	33.0			
22	563	32.7			
12	29,115	25.2			

Male Subsets With No Females

Sufficient Number to Model			Small Subsets		
Subset Code	N	Denial Rate (%)*	Subset Code	N	Denial Rate (%)
13	1,012	37.1	31	52	32.7
15	26,009	33.4			
11	490	26.5			

* Test of null hypothesis of joint equality of denial rates across subsets: $\chi^2 = 16.38$, P value = 0.00.

Lending Examination Procedures, 50 approvals and 50 denials per group are needed to conduct statistical modeling.[9] Subsets with smaller volumes are listed in adjacent columns. Subsets that do not meet the 50/50 threshold but have at least 30 applications are presented first, followed by subsets with fewer than 30 applications. Based on the OCC's *Sampling Methodology Handbook*, at least 30 applications are needed to calculate reliable statistics.[10] Therefore, denial rates are presented for subsets with at least 30 applications. For subsets with fewer than 30 applications, only the number denied is presented.

As presented in table 8, for Black applicants, four underlying subsets have at least 50 approvals and 50 denials, three do not meet the 50/50 threshold but have at least 30 applications, and 31 have fewer than 30 applications. Consistent with earlier results, the subsets with the largest volumes are single applicants and joint applications in which both applicants are Black. The subsets with the smallest volumes consist primarily of mixed applications. Looking at table 9, the dataset contains applications for seven of the eight possible Hispanic subsets. Five of these subsets have sufficient numbers of applications for modeling, one does not have sufficient volume for modeling but has at least 30 applications, and one has fewer than 30 applications. The subset consisting of joint applications in which the primary applicant reports NA and the coapplicant reports Hispanic is the one subset with no applications. For females, data are available for six of the eight possible subsets, as shown in table 10. Five of these subsets have at least 50 approvals and 50 denials and one does not meet the 50/50 threshold but has at least 30

---

[9] See the OCC's *Fair Lending Examination Procedures: Comptroller's Handbook* (April 2006).

[10] See the OCC's *Sampling Methodologies Comptroller's Handbook* (August 1998).

applications. The subsets consisting of joint applications in which one applicant reports female and the other reports NA are the two subsets with no applications.

Step 2: Identify Control Groups

The second step is to identify the comparison groups for the analysis. We impose just one criterion, that a comparison group must only contain applications that only report that group. This differs slightly from treatment of minorities in which an application is considered a potential for a minority group if that minority is reported anywhere in the application.

Tables 8-10 list all subsets for White applicants, non-Hispanics, and males, respectively. These are the potential comparison groups for the analysis. For White applicants, there are six possible subsets that contain only White applications. As table 8 shows, data are available for four of these subsets and all four meet the threshold of 50 approvals and 50 denials. The subsets of joint applications in which one applicant reports White and the other reports NA are the two subsets with no applications. For non-Hispanics, there are six possible subsets with only non-Hispanic applications.

As listed in table 9, data are available for five of these subsets. Four subsets meet the 50/50 threshold and one has fewer than 30 applications. The subset of joint applications in which the primary applicant is non-Hispanic and the coapplicant reports NA is the one subset with no applications. For males, there are six possible subsets that contain only male applicants. As listed in table 10, data are available for four of these six subsets with three meeting the 50/50 threshold and the fourth meeting the at-least-30-applications threshold. The subsets of joint applications in which one applicant reports male and the other reports NA are the two subsets with no applications.

For a given ethnic, racial, or gender analysis, the underlying subsets comprising non-Hispanic, White, and male should be combined into composite control groups. All subsets should be included here, regardless of the number of applications. These composite control groups should be used during every disparity analysis. In addition, using the data-driven approach advocated here, statistical tests should determine whether the underlying subsets should be used separately as control groups. As tables 8-10 indicate, there is considerable variation across these subsets, which might suggest systematic differences in the characteristics of these subsets or in the treatment of these subsets. For White applicants, the denial rates range from 26.3 to 33.2 percent. For non-Hispanics and males, the denial rates range from 26.8 to 37.2 percent and 26.5 to 37.1 percent, respectively. Included in the tables are tests of the null hypothesis of joint equality of denial rates across subsets. A Wald test is used and all subsets with at least 30 applications are included in the tests. If the null hypothesis of equality is rejected, each underlying subset with at least 50 approvals and 50 denials should be analyzed as a separate control group as well. If the null hypothesis cannot be rejected, then only the composite group should be used. As the results in Tables 8-10 show, the null hypothesis of joint equality can be rejected in all three instances.[11] Based on these results, in addition to the composite version of each control variable, we also use each underlying subset separately as the control group.

---

[11] This testing could be expanded to pairwise tests to find pairs of groups that could be combined. For White applicants, pairwise tests rejected equality of denial rates for the following pairs of subsets, (5000060000, 5000050000) and (5000080000, 5000050000). For non-Hispanics, pairwise tests rejected equality of denial rates for the following pairs of subsets, (23, 25), (23, 32), (23, 22), and (24, 22). For males, pairwise tests rejected equality of denial rates for the following pairs of subsets, (13, 15), (13, 11), and (15, 11).

Step 3: Disparity Analysis Using Subsets With Sufficient Volume for Modeling

The next step is to analyze disparities for minority subsets with sufficient numbers of applications for modeling. All minority subsets with fewer than 50 approvals and 50 denials are excluded from the analysis for now. Separate disparity analyses are conducted for ethnicity, race, and gender. For each of these analyses, separate models are estimated for each control group and the complete set of minority subsets is included in each model. For example, for the ethnicity analysis, five models are estimated; one using the composite non-Hispanic group as the control group, and four using each of the underlying non-Hispanic subsets listed in table 9 as the control group. All five Hispanic subsets listed in table 9 are included in each of these models. For all estimations, the model specification from the actual examination is used and a logit estimator is used to estimate all models.

For an actual fair lending analysis, the objective at this point would be to test for disparate treatment. However, for confidentiality reasons, we focus only on variation in estimated disparities across minority subsets. Using a Wald test, we test the null hypothesis that the coefficients on the minority subsets jointly equal 0. Table 11 presents the Wald test results (χ^2 statistic and *P* value), the minority subset with the highest estimated marginal effect, the subset with the lowest estimated marginal effect, and the range of estimated marginal effects across the underlying minority subsets.[12] Results are presented for the composite control group and each subset control group.

---

[12] To calculate the range of marginal effects, we first calculate, for each subset, the average predicted probability of denial as if all applicants belonged to that subset. The range is the difference between the highest and lowest average predicted probabilities. For all of these calculations, the actual data for all other variables are used.

Table 11: Disparity Analysis Using Examination Data					
Race (Black Subsets, n = 4)					
Control Subset	Subset With Highest Marginal Effect	Subset With Lowest Marginal Effect	Range of Marginal Effects	Wald Test of Joint Equality of Marginal Effects	
				χ^2 Statistic	P Value
Composite	3000050000	3000060000	0.071	4.00	0.26
5000060000	3000050000	3000060000	0.062	3.12	0.37
5000080000	3000050000	3000060000	0.074	4.13	0.25
6000050000	3000050000	3000060000	0.062	3.05	0.38
5000050000	3000050000	3000060000	0.064	3.57	0.31
Ethnicity (Hispanic Subsets, n = 5)					
Control Subset	Subset With Highest Marginal Effect	Subset With Lowest Marginal Effect	Range of Marginal Effects	Wald Test of Joint Equality of Marginal Effects	
				χ^2 Statistic	P Value
Composite	13	21	0.066	12.77	0.01
23	13	21	0.060	11.25	0.02
25	13	21	0.061	12.29	0.02
32	13	21	0.056	10.60	0.03
22	13	21	0.068	13.52	0.01
Gender (Female Subsets, n = 5)					
Control Subset	Subset With Highest Marginal Effect	Subset With Lowest Marginal Effect	Range of Marginal Effects	Wald Test of Joint Equality of Marginal Effects	
				χ^2 Statistic	P Value
Composite	22	12	0.037	49.17	0.00
13	23	12	0.037	51.76	0.00
15	22	12	0.037	49.02	0.00
11	23	12	0.037	51.62	0.00

There are a number of interesting results in table 11. First, even after accounting for the legitimate factors this lender considered when underwriting loan applications, there is significant variation in the estimated marginal effects across minority subsets. Looking at the composite results, the range of estimated marginal effects is 7.1, 6.6, and 3.7 percent for Blacks, Hispanics, and females, respectively. For ethnicity and gender, the null hypothesis of joint equality of marginal effects is rejected at the 95 percent confidence level, as indicated in the table by P values of less than 0.05. This variation suggests that these underlying minority groups should be analyzed separately.[13]

Second, the estimated marginal effects and the Wald test results vary little across the various non-minority subsets used as the control group. The biggest difference is 1.2 percent, which occurred for both ethnicity (control subsets 32 and 22) and race (control subsets 5000080000 and both 6000050000 and 5000060000). Therefore, for this examination, the data suggest that it would be sufficient to use the composite group as the control group.

Third, accounting for legitimate underwriting factors affects the relative risk-levels across minority subsets for race and gender, but not ethnicity. For race, joint applications in which the primary applicant is Black and the coapplicant is White showed the smallest raw denial rate (table 8). However, this subset shows the highest estimated marginal effect after considering legitimate underwriting factors. For gender, joint applications from two females have one of the lowest raw denial rates (table 10). However, this subset has the highest estimated marginal effect in two instances in table

---

[13] These types of conclusions depend on the reliability of the estimated statistical model. As with any analysis, the results are less reliable to the extent that issues such as omitted variables, multicollinearity, or heteroskadasticity affect the statistical models.

11. For ethnicity, the subsets showing the highest and lowest raw denial rates in table 9 also show the highest and lowest estimated marginal effects in table 11.

Finally, it is interesting to note that mixed-ethnic joint applications in which non-Hispanic is listed as the primary applicant, and mixed-gender joint applications in which male is listed as the primary applicant, consistently show the smallest estimated marginal effects.

Following a data-driven approach, the results in table 11 suggest using minority subsets for both ethnicity and gender, aggregating minority subsets for race, and using composite control groups for ethnicity, race, and gender. Overall, the results in this section suggest that the underlying subsets of aggregate ethnic, racial, and gender groups should be analyzed separately.

Step 4: Incorporate Small Sample Minority Subsets Into the Analysis

The final step is to incorporate into the analysis minority subsets with low volumes. Because these subsets have insufficient numbers of observations for modeling, some aggregation is needed. To minimize the amount of judgment we interject into the analysis, we employ a conservative aggregation strategy based only on the ordering of reported ethnicity, race, and gender values in HMDA. Up to this point, the order of values in the ethnicity, race, and gender variables matters. We now relax this criterion. For example, a joint application with a Black primary applicant and an Asian coapplicant is categorized into a different subset than a joint applicant with an Asian primary applicant and a Black coapplicant. These two applications would now be combined into the same subset.[14]

For all minority subsets with small samples, applications are aggregated up to subsets with similar sets of values. To convey this process, we discuss the racial, ethnic, and gender analyses one at a time. Table 12 presents the results of this aggregation for Black applicants. The first four columns transcribe the subsets with small samples from Table 8.

---

[14] We treat the "no coapplicant" value as a valid value. This is especially relevant for race, because each applicant can report up to five races. For example, the racial subset code for a single applicant who reports both Black and Asian would be 2300080000, in which the 8 indicates that there is no coapplicant. A joint application in which one applicant is Black and the other Asian would be coded as 2000030000, which would continue to be a separate subset.

Table 12: Aggregation of Small Subsets of the Aggregate Black Group

	Underlying Subsets				Aggregate Subsets		
Subset	N	Number of Denials	Denial Rate (%)	Subset	N	Number of Denials	Denial Rate (%)
3000013000	2	2	NA	13	12	8	NA
1300030000	1	1	NA	13			
1300013000	1	1	NA	13			
3000010000	4	3	NA	13			
1000030000	4	1	NA	13			
3000020000	17	4	NA	23	29	10	NA
2000030000	12	6	NA	23			
4000030000	7	3	NA	34	16	5	NA
3000040000	9	2	NA	34			
5000030000	135	39	28.9	35	175	51	29.1
3500035000	15	8	NA	35			
3500050000	5	2	NA	35			
5000035000	10	2	NA	35			
5000053000	1	0	NA	35			
3500030000	4	0	NA	35			
5300053000	1	0	NA	35			
3000035000	4	0	NA	35			
6000030000	41	13	31.7	36	41	13	31.7
1300050000	1	1	NA	135	6	3	NA
5000013000	1	1	NA	135			
3500013000	2	1	NA	135			
1350050000	1	0	NA	135			
1500013500	1	0	NA	135			
1300080000	7	6	NA	138	7	6	NA
2350023500	1	1	NA	235	3	2	NA
5000023000	2	1	NA	235			
2300080000	2	1	NA	238	2	1	NA
3500040000	1	1	NA	345	1	1	NA
3400080000	3	3	NA	348	3	3	NA
6000035000	1	1	NA	356	1	1	NA
3500080000	45	23	51.1	358	47	25	53.2
5300080000	2	2	NA	358			
1350080000	2	1	NA	1358	2	1	NA
3450080000	1	0	NA	3458	1	0	NA

The final four columns show the newly aggregated subsets along with the number of applications, number of denials, and, for subsets with at least 30 applications, the denial rate. As the table shows, the original 31 subsets are reduced to 15.

Table 12 contains four subsets of interest. First, the subset consisting of joint applications with a Black and White applicant (subset code 35) now has sufficient volume for modeling. Aggregation in this instance seems appropriate, because the denial rate changed only slightly—from 28.9 to 29.1 percent. Second, should this new aggregate subset be a separate subset in the regression analysis or should we combine it with one of the original subsets that had sufficient volume for modeling? In this example, there is one such subset that is a potential for further aggregation, the subset consisting of joint applications in which the primary applicant is Black and the coapplicant is White. A t-test could not reject the null hypothesis that the denial rates for these two subsets are equal. Based on this evidence, we combine these two subsets into one.

In this example, there is only one possible subset suitable for aggregation. If the original list of subsets with sufficient volume contains multiple subsets that could be combined with a new aggregate subset, conduct a test of joint equality of denial rates. If joint equality cannot be rejected, then combine all subsets into one. If joint equality can be rejected, then conduct pairwise t-tests to determine which subsets can be combined, if any, and which subsets should enter the model separately.

A second subset of interest in table 12 is subset 36. Although this subset does not meet the 50/50 threshold, it does contain 30 applications, so the denial rate is reliable. Looking at the original list of subsets with sufficient volume to include in modeling, there is one subset that is a potential for aggregation—the subset of joint applications in which the primary applicant is Black and the coapplicant reports "Internet, mail, telephone." A *t*-test could not reject the null hypothesis that the denial rates for these two subsets are equal. Therefore, we combine these two subsets into one.

A third subset of interest in table 12 is subset 358. Looking at the original list of subsets with sufficient volume for modeling, there are no subsets that are potentials for aggregation. In this example, the newly aggregated subset does not have sufficient applications to be included as a separate subset for modeling. Therefore, this subset would need to be reviewed outside the modeling analysis. Because it contains at least 30 applications, denial rate disparities can be constructed with the composite and subset control groups. These denial rate disparities range from 1.60 to 2.02 and all are statistically significant at the 95 percent confidence level. These results suggest higher fair lending risk for this subset, so a review of files may be necessary.

The final subset or subsets of interest are the 12 remaining subsets in table 12 with fewer than 30 applications. Statistically, there is little that can be done with these subsets, given their small volumes and the current sample size requirements at the OCC. Fortunately, there are few of these applications. In total, these 12 subsets contain only 85 applications. Although we narrow the number of excluded applications to a small number, a review of these files may still be needed to verify that no fair lending issues exist.

Having completed the aggregation of small sample subsets for Black applicants, we now move on to Hispanics and females. Incorporating the small sample subsets for Hispanics and females is considerably easier, because there are far fewer subsets. As presented in table 9, there are two small sample subsets for Hispanics. The first, joint applications in which the primary applicant reports "Internet, mail, telephone," and the coapplicant is Hispanic, can be combined with only one subset, joint applications in which the primary applicant is Hispanic and the coapplicant reports "Internet, mail, telephone." A t-test could not reject the null hypothesis that the denial rate for these two subsets is equal at the 95 percent confidence level. Therefore, these subsets are combined.

The second Hispanic subset with small volume is joint applications in which the primary applicant is Hispanic and the coapplicant reported NA. There are no groups with sufficient volume for modeling that can be combined with this subset. Further, because there is only one application for this subset, denial rate disparities cannot be constructed. A review of this file may be needed to verify that no fair lending issues exist.

For Hispanics, we also need to test the null hypothesis of equality of denial rates for subsets 21 and 12. Though both of these subsets have sufficient volumes to be included in the modeling analysis, we need to test for possible aggregation possibilities to be consistent with the overall aggregation approach we are using. A t-test could not reject the null hypothesis that the denial rate for these two subsets is equal at the 95 percent confidence level. Therefore, these subsets are combined as well.

For gender, there is only one subset for females with small volume—joint applications in which the primary applicant reported "Internet, mail, telephone" and the coapplicant is female. This group may be combined with joint applications in which the primary applicant is female and the coapplicant reported "Internet, mail, telephone." This latter group has sufficient volume for modeling. A t-test could not reject the null hypothesis that the denial rates for these two subsets are equal at the 95 percent confidence level. Based on this evidence, we combine these two subsets for the regression analysis.

For females, we also need to test the null hypothesis of equality of denial rates for subsets 21 and 12. Though both of these subsets have sufficient volumes to be included in the modeling analysis, we need to test for possible aggregation possibilities to be consistent with the overall aggregation approach we are using. A *t*-test rejected the null hypothesis that the denial rate for these two subsets is equal at the 95 percent confidence level. Therefore, these subsets continue to enter the regression models separately.

Based on this final step, five changes were made that affect the modeling analysis. Two new aggregate ethnic subsets were formed, two new aggregate racial subsets were formed, and one new aggregate gender subset was formed. With these new subsets, we re-estimated all models to update the results from table 11. Table 13 presents these results. For ethnicity, the affects of aggregation are fairly minor. The subsets with the highest and lowest estimated marginal effects are the same and the range of estimated marginal effects dropped only slightly. The *P* values on the Wald tests increase slightly as well, but all test statistics are still statistically significant at the 90 percent confidence level. The effects on the racial results are very similar. The range of estimated marginal effects decreases slightly and the *P* values increase. The gender results are basically unchanged. This is not surprising, because aggregating gender subsets 23 and 32 is a relatively minor adjustment.

The minor differences between the results in tables 11 and 13 suggest that the aggregation we imposed is appropriate. If the results had changed dramatically, further

Table 13: Post-Aggregation Disparity Analysis Using Examination Data

Race (Black Subsets, n = 4)

Control Subset	Subset With Highest Marginal Effect	Subset With Lowest Marginal Effect	Range of Marginal Effects	Wald Test of Joint Equality of Marginal Effects	
				χ^2 Statistic	P Value
Composite	All 35s	All 36s	0.031	1.46	0.69
5000060000	All 35s	All 36s	0.025	1.08	0.78
5000080000	All 35s	All 36s	0.034	1.37	0.71
6000050000	All 35s	All 36s	0.026	0.92	0.82
5000050000	All 35s	All 36s	0.026	1.30	0.73

Ethnicity (Hispanic Subsets, n = 4)

Control Subset	Subset With Highest Marginal Effect	Subset With Lowest Marginal Effect	Range of Marginal Effects	Wald Test of Joint Equality of Marginal Effects	
				χ^2 Statistic	P Value
Composite	13 and 31	12 and 21	0.042	8.60	0.04
23	13 and 31	12 and 21	0.038	7.53	0.06
25	13 and 31	12 and 21	0.039	8.39	0.04
32	13 and 31	12 and 21	0.035	6.85	0.08
22	13 and 31	12 and 21	0.045	9.09	0.03

Gender (Female Subsets, n = 5)

Control Subset	Subset With Highest Marginal Effect	Subset With Lowest Marginal Effect	Range of Marginal Effects	Wald Test of Joint Equality of Marginal Effects	
				χ^2 Statistic	P Value
Composite	22	12	0.037	49.39	0.00
13	22	12	0.037	52.11	0.00
15	22	12	0.037	49.23	0.00
11	22	12	0.036	51.96	0.00

analysis would have been needed to determine the cause. In such a situation, aggregation may turn out not to be appropriate.

As noted, because of confidentiality reasons, we could not focus the discussion in this section on identifying the ethnic, racial, and gender groups with the highest fair lending risk. During an actual analysis, however, this would be the focus. Once the four steps of the data-driven approach are complete, the results would be analyzed to identify the subset or subsets showing statistically significant disparities. Consistent with the standard risk-based approach to fair lending analyses, further analyses and possibly a file review of these subsets would then be undertaken.

VI. Conclusion

Discrimination in credit markets, if it exists, occurs during interactions between individuals. One individual, such as a loan officer, attempts to disadvantage a credit applicant based on a dislike of certain characteristics of that applicant. Some characteristics that may initiate discriminatory behavior include ethnicity, gender, skin color, skin shade, clothing, speech, or hygiene. In addition to characteristics of the applicant, the characteristics and experiences of the loan officer likely affect treatment of the applicant as well. All of these possible influences make it difficult to isolate a discriminatory effect to a single characteristic, such as race, ethnicity, or gender. Data to account for all the other possible characteristics that may influence interactions is simply not available. Given these complexities, imposing a judgmental classification structure to group applicants only adds to the uncertainty of the analysis. If the classification structure imposed on the data differs from the true form of discriminatory behavior, true underlying patterns of discriminatory behavior may be masked or distorted.

In this study, we present a data-driven approach to classify applicants, which minimizes the judgment interjected by the analyst. Using HMDA data from 2005, we analyze variation in denial rates across base subsets of data that comprise the typical aggregate ethnic, racial, and gender groups used for fair lending analyses. We then use a dataset from a fair lending examination the OCC recently conducted to show how a data-driven approach would be applied during an actual analysis. The empirical results provide many examples in which the variation in denial rates is high. Such variation suggests that the applicants in these underlying subsets have systematically different characteristics or are receiving systematically different treatment. Either way, these groups should be analyzed separately.

The Equal Credit Opportunity Act states that lenders cannot consider race, ethnicity, and gender in any way during credit transactions. A data-driven classification strategy, which mines data for any patterns showing race, ethnicity, and gender being used in any way, is consistent with the spirit of the Act.

References

Aspinall, Peter J., 1997, "The Conceptual Basis of Ethnic Group Terminology and Classifications," *Social Science Medicine*, Vol. 45, No. 5, 689-698.

Bell, Carolyn Shaw, 1996, "Data on Race, Ethnicity, and Gender: Caveats for the User," *International Labour Review,* Vol. 135, No. 5, 535-551.

Campbell, Mary E., 2007, "Thinking Outside the (Black) Box: Measuring Black and Multiracial Identification on Surveys," *Social Science Research*, Vol. 36, 921-944.

Executive Office of the President, Office of Management and Budget, 1997, "OMB Revisions to the Standards for the Classification of Federal Data on Race and Ethnicity," October 30, 1997,

http://www.whitehouse.gov/omb/fedreg/ombdir15.html

Federal Financial Institutions Examination Council, 2009, "A Guide to HMDA Reporting: Getting It Right!"

Hirschman, Charles, Richard Alba, and Reynolds Farley, 2000, "The Meaning and Measurement of Race in the U.S. Census: Glimpses Into the Future," *Demography,* Vol. 37, No. 3, 381-393.

Holloway, Steven R. and Elvin K. Wyly, 2002, "The Disappearance of Race in Mortgage Lending," *Economic Geography,* Vol. 78, No. 2, 129-169.

Huck, Paul, 2001, "Home Mortgage Lending by Applicant Race: Do HMDA Figures Provide a Distorted Picture?" *Housing Policy Debate*, Vol. 12, No. 4, 719-736.

James, Angela, 2001, "Making Sense of Race and Racial Classification," *Race and Society*, Vol. 4, 235-247.

Office of the Comptroller of the Currency, April 2006, "Fair Lending Examination Procedures: Comptroller's Handbook."

Office of the Comptroller of the Currency, August 1998, "Sampling Methodologies: Comptroller's Handbook."

Robbin, Alice, 1999, "The Problematic Status of U.S. Statistics on Race and Ethnicity: An Imperfect Representation of Reality," *Journal of Government Information,* Vol. 26, No. 5, 467-483.

Saperstein, Aliya, 2006, "Double-Checking the Race Box: Examining Inconsistency Between Survey Measures of Observed and Self-Reported Race," *Social Forces,* Vol. 85, No. 1, 58-74.

Williams, David R., 1999, "The Monitoring of Racial/Ethnic Status in the USA: Data Quality Issues," *Ethnicity and Health*, Vol. 4, No. 3: 121-137.

Appendix: Breakdown of Ethnic, Racial, and Gender Groups Into Base Subsets (Number of applications and denial rates)*

Table A1a: Number of Applications for American Indians, by Lender and Subset Code

Lender	1000010000	1000050000	1000080000	1300080000	1350080000	1500050000	1500015000	1500080000
1	1230	268	2230	50	33	122	127	357
5	55	0	86	0	0	0	0	0
8	0	0	32	0	0	0	0	0
10	136	73	460	0	0	0	0	0
13	276	136	861	0	0	0	35	76
16	0	0	105	0	0	0	0	0
18	159	0	296	0	0	0	0	0
19	856	425	1481	0	0	0	51	90
21	31	0	35	0	0	0	0	0
22	195	48	717	0	0	0	0	45

Lender	5000010000	5000015000	1000060000	5000080000	5000051000	5100050000	5100051000	5100080000
1	283	122	0	0	0	0	0	0
5	0	0	0	0	0	0	0	0
8	0	0	0	0	0	0	0	0
10	60	0	0	0	0	0	0	0
13	125	34	30	0	0	0	0	0
16	0	0	0	0	0	0	0	0
18	0	0	0	0	0	0	0	0
19	420	55	0	0	51	60	37	95
21	0	0	0	0	0	0	0	0
22	41	0	0	0	0	0	0	0

* Note: Throughout the appendix tables, column headings represent subset codes, which are explained in the Summary of the Data-Driven Approach section.

Table A1b: Percent Denied for American Indians, by Lender and Subset Code

Lender	1000010000	1000050000	1000080000	1300080000	1350080000	1500015000
1	38.21	27.61	43.99	58	33.33	36.89
5	9.09	0.00	22.09	0	0.00	0.00
8	0.00	0.00	9.38	0	0.00	0.00
10	13.24	9.59	18.70	0	0.00	0.00
13	18.12	13.97	19.05	0	0.00	0.00
16	0.00	0.00	43.81	0	0.00	0.00
18	24.53	0.00	30.07	0	0.00	0.00
19	14.14	13.18	19.18	0	0.00	0.00
21	3.23	0.00	8.57	0	0.00	0.00
22	73.33	68.75	68.76	0	0.00	0.00

Lender	1500050000	1500080000	5000010000	5000015000	1000060000
1	30.71	40.06	26.15	30.33	0.00
5	0.00	0.00	0.00	0.00	0.00
8	0.00	0.00	0.00	0.00	0.00
10	0.00	0.00	18.33	0.00	0.00
13	17.14	11.84	12.80	20.59	13.33
16	0.00	0.00	0.00	0.00	0.00
18	0.00	0.00	0.00	0.00	0.00
19	13.73	12.22	13.33	14.55	0.00
21	0.00	0.00	0.00	0.00	0.00
22	0.00	66.67	56.10	0.00	0.00

Lender	5000051000	5100050000	5100051000	5100080000
1	0.00	0.00	0.00	0
5	0.00	0.00	0.00	0
8	0.00	0.00	0.00	0
10	0.00	0.00	0.00	0
13	0.00	0.00	0.00	0
16	0.00	0.00	0.00	0
18	0.00	0.00	0.00	0
19	21.57	21.67	10.81	20
21	0.00	0.00	0.00	0
22	0.00	0.00	0.00	0

Table A2a: Number of Applications for Asians, by Lender and Subset Code

Lender	2000020000	2000030000	2000050000	2000060000	2000080000	2400080000	2500020000
1	10081	35	923	66	13543	48	35
3	54	0	0	0	82	0	0
4	0	0	0	0	51	0	0
5	403	0	37	0	418	0	0
7	54	0	0	0	63	0	0
8	1513	0	69	0	3131	0	0
9	94	0	0	0	129	0	0
10	3580	0	266	0	7693	0	0
13	3271	0	357	97	6144	0	0
15	30	0	0	0	33	0	0
16	567	0	79	0	940	0	0
17	115	0	0	0	119	0	0
18	597	0	74	0	929	0	0
19	11534	49	1363	133	15447	40	0
20	33	0	0	0	33	0	0
21	303	0	0	0	345	0	0
22	2266	0	132	92	7997	0	0

Lender	2500025000	2500050000	2500080000	3000020000	4000020000	5000020000	5000025000
1	35	67	192	47	36	1461	55
3	0	0	0	0	0	0	0
4	0	0	0	0	0	0	0
5	0	0	0	0	0	48	0
7	0	0	0	0	0	0	0
8	0	0	0	0	0	108	0
9	0	0	0	0	0	0	0
10	0	0	42	0	0	459	0
13	0	0	87	49	0	550	40
15	0	0	0	0	0	0	0
16	0	0	0	0	0	106	0
17	0	0	0	0	0	0	0
18	0	0	0	0	0	113	0
19	0	49	92	90	31	2215	55
20	0	0	0	0	0	0	0
21	0	0	0	0	0	31	0
22	0	0	85	0	0	207	0

Table A2a: Number of Applications for Asians, by Lender and Subset Code (cont'd.)

Lender	6000020C000	2000040000	5000052000	5200020000	5200050000	5200052000	5200080000
1	33	0	0	0	0	0	0
3	0	0	0	0	0	0	0
4	0	0	0	0	0	0	0
5	0	0	0	0	0	0	0
7	0	0	0	0	0	0	0
8	0	0	0	0	0	0	0
9	0	0	0	0	0	0	0
10	47	0	0	0	0	0	0
13	0	0	0	0	0	0	0
15	0	0	0	0	0	0	0
16	0	0	0	0	0	0	0
17	0	0	0	0	0	0	0
18	0	0	0	0	0	0	0
19	69	35	39	47	47	45	114
20	0	0	0	0	0	0	0
21	0	0	0	0	0	0	0
22	0	0	0	0	0	0	0

Table A2b: Percent Denied for Asians, by Lender and Subset Code

Lender	2000020000	2000030000	2000050000	2000060000	2000080000	2400080000
1	19.35	28.57	13.76	18.18	21.86	37.5
3	1.85	0.00	0.00	0.00	6.10	0.0
4	0.00	0.00	0.00	0.00	3.92	0.0
5	3.23	0.00	8.11	0.00	9.81	0.0
7	5.56	0.00	0.00	0.00	9.52	0.0
8	4.23	0.00	10.14	0.00	6.26	0.0
9	5.32	0.00	0.00	0.00	9.30	0.0
10	16.62	0.00	15.04	0.00	15.55	0.0
13	11.43	0.00	6.72	17.53	16.19	0.0
15	6.67	0.00	0.00	0.00	12.12	0.0
16	13.05	0.00	5.06	0.00	20.43	0.0
17	12.17	0.00	0.00	0.00	15.13	0.0
18	14.91	0.00	8.11	0.00	16.79	0.0
19	7.01	18.37	6.31	15.04	10.01	22.5
20	21.21	0.00	0.00	0.00	24.24	0.0
21	7.92	0.00	0.00	0.00	7.25	0.0
22	49.51	0.00	59.09	57.61	51.53	0.0

Lender	2500020000	2500025000	2500050000	2500080000	3000020000	4000020000
1	17.14	22.86	25.37	23.96	38.30	19.44
3	0.00	0.00	0.00	0.00	0.00	0.00
4	0.00	0.00	0.00	0.00	0.00	0.00
5	0.00	0.00	0.00	0.00	0.00	0.00
7	0.00	0.00	0.00	0.00	0.00	0.00
8	0.00	0.00	0.00	0.00	0.00	0.00
9	0.00	0.00	0.00	0.00	0.00	0.00
10	0.00	0.00	0.00	16.67	0.00	0.00
13	0.00	0.00	0.00	10.34	18.37	0.00
15	0.00	0.00	0.00	0.00	0.00	0.00
16	0.00	0.00	0.00	0.00	0.00	0.00
17	0.00	0.00	0.00	0.00	0.00	0.00
18	0.00	0.00	0.00	0.00	0.00	0.00
19	0.00	0.00	6.12	15.22	7.78	0.00
20	0.00	0.00	0.00	0.00	0.00	0.00
21	0.00	0.00	0.00	0.00	0.00	0.00
22	0.00	0.00	0.00	67.06	0.00	0.00

Table A2b: Percent Denied for Asians, by Lender and Subset Code (cont'd.)

Lender	5000020000	5000025000	6000020000	2000040000	5000052000	5200020000
1	11.91	25.45	36.36	0.00	0.00	0.00
3	C.00	0.00	0.00	0.00	0.00	0.00
4	C.00	0.00	0.00	0.00	0.00	0.00
5	4.17	0.00	0.00	0.00	0.00	0.00
7	0.00	0.00	0.00	0.00	0.00	0.00
8	3.70	0.00	0.00	0.00	0.00	0.00
9	0.00	0.00	0.00	0.00	0.00	0.00
10	13.29	0.00	0.00	0.00	0.00	0.00
13	8.91	7.50	12.77	0.00	0.00	0.00
15	0.00	0.00	0.00	0.00	0.00	0.00
16	10.38	0.00	0.00	0.00	0.00	0.00
17	0.00	0.00	0.00	0.00	0.00	0.00
18	6.19	0.00	0.00	0.00	0.00	0.00
19	5.10	20.00	15.94	5.71	10.26	6.38
20	0.00	0.00	0.00	0.00	0.00	0.00
21	9.68	0.00	0.00	0.00	0.00	0.00
22	56.04	0.00	0.00	0.00	0.00	0.00

Lender	5200050000	5200052000	5200080000
1	0.00	0.00	0.00
3	0.00	0.00	0.00
4	0.00	0.00	0.00
5	0.00	0.00	0.00
7	0.00	0.00	0.00
8	0.00	0.00	0.00
9	0.00	0.00	0.00
10	0.00	0.00	0.00
13	0.00	0.00	0.00
15	0.00	0.00	0.00
16	0.00	0.00	0.00
17	0.00	0.00	0.00
18	0.00	0.00	0.00
19	10.64	4.44	9.65
20	0.00	0.00	0.00
21	0.00	0.00	0.00
22	0.00	0.00	0.00

Table A3a: Number of Applications for Black Applicants, by Lender and Subset Code

Lender	1300080000	1350080000	2000030000	3000020000	3000030000	3000050000	3000060000
1	50	33	35	47	5337	442	66
3	0	0	0	0	105	0	0
4	0	0	0	0	0	0	0
5	0	0	0	0	180	0	0
7	0	0	0	0	41	0	0
8	0	0	0	0	391	43	0
9	0	0	0	0	123	30	0
10	0	0	0	0	1569	163	0
11	0	0	0	0	48	0	0
13	0	0	0	49	4876	423	245
14	0	0	0	0	0	0	0
15	0	0	0	0	0	0	0
16	0	0	0	0	420	57	0
18	0	0	0	0	968	75	0
19	0	0	49	90	5426	814	113
21	0	0	0	0	86	0	0
22	0	0	0	0	497	82	0

Lender	3000080000	3500080000	5000030000	6000030000	3000070000	5300080000
1	15442	129	379	32	0	0
3	287	0	0	0	0	0
4	100	0	0	0	0	0
5	740	0	0	0	0	0
7	134	0	0	0	0	0
8	1111	0	0	0	0	0
9	510	0	139	0	0	0
10	4987	0	0	0	42	0
11	220	0	0	0	0	0
13	19791	113	315	64	0	0
14	111	0	0	0	0	0
15	34	0	0	0	0	0
16	1807	0	40	0	0	0
18	3217	0	122	0	0	0
19	15366	68	540	37	0	62
21	191	0	0	0	0	0
22	2442	33	45	0	0	0

Table A3b: Percent Denied for Black Applicants, by Lender and Subset Code

Lender	1300080000	1350080000	2000030000	3000020000	3000030000	3000050000	3000060000
1	58	33.33	28.57	38.30	36.99	29.86	42.42
3	0	0.00	0.00	0.00	7.62	0.00	0.00
4	0	0.00	0.00	0.00	0.00	0.00	0.00
5	0	0.00	0.00	0.00	12.22	0.00	0.00
7	0	0.00	0.00	0.00	17.07	0.00	0.00
8	0	0.00	0.00	0.00	16.37	9.30	0.00
9	0	0.00	0.00	0.00	13.01	26.67	0.00
10	0	0.00	0.00	0.00	21.73	17.79	0.00
11	0	0.00	0.00	0.00	22.92	0.00	0.00
13	0	0.00	0.00	18.37	17.35	11.82	22.45
14	0	0.00	0.00	0.00	0.00	0.00	0.00
15	0	0.00	0.00	0.00	0.00	0.00	0.00
16	0	0.00	0.00	0.00	43.10	33.33	0.00
18	0	0.00	0.00	0.00	19.52	5.33	0.00
19	0	0.00	18.37	7.78	17.67	12.78	19.47
21	0	0.00	0.00	0.00	6.98	0.00	0.00
22	0	0.00	0.00	0.00	58.55	54.88	0.00

Lender	3000080000	3500080000	5000030000	6000030000	3000070000	5300080000
1	38.10	36.43	27.70	43.75	0.00	0.00
3	12.89	0.00	0.00	0.00	0.00	0.00
4	11.00	0.00	0.00	0.00	0.00	0.00
5	25.54	0.00	0.00	0.00	0.00	0.00
7	17.91	0.00	0.00	0.00	0.00	0.00
8	14.49	0.00	0.00	0.00	0.00	0.00
9	21.37	0.00	0.00	0.00	0.00	0.00
10	25.01	0.00	17.99	0.00	11.90	0.00
11	31.82	0.00	0.00	0.00	0.00	0.00
13	19.70	14.16	13.02	23.44	0.00	0.00
14	23.42	0.00	0.00	0.00	0.00	0.00
15	14.71	0.00	0.00	0.00	0.00	0.00
16	48.64	0.00	35.00	0.00	0.00	0.00
18	21.76	0.00	5.74	0.00	0.00	0.00
19	24.99	30.88	13.15	16.22	0.00	27.42
21	13.61	0.00	0.00	0.00	0.00	0.00
22	64.95	69.70	57.78	0.00	0.00	0.00

Table A4a: Number of Applications for Native Hawaiians, by Lender and Subset Code

Lender	2400080000	4000020000	4000040000	4000050000	4000080000
1	48	36	921	177	1426
5	0	0	0	0	36
8	0	0	0	0	71
10	0	0	141	52	358
13	0	0	337	124	708
16	0	0	30	0	76
18	0	0	67	0	137
19	40	31	756	312	969
22	0	0	207	36	435

Lender	4500080000	5000040000	4000060000	5000045000	2000040000
1	46	233	0	0	0
5	0	0	0	0	0
8	0	0	0	0	0
10	0	61	0	0	0
13	58	120	32	30	0
16	0	0	0	0	0
18	0	0	0	0	0
19	32	325	0	0	35
22	0	45	0	0	0

Table A4b: Percent Denied Native Hawaiians, by Lender and Subset Code

Lender	2400080000	4000020000	4000040000	4000050000	4000080000
1	37.5	19.44	33.22	15.25	42.08
5	0.0	0.00	0.00	0.00	27.78
8	0.0	0.00	0.00	0.00	15.49
10	0.0	0.00	21.28	19.23	18.99
13	0.0	0.00	13.65	13.71	15.54
16	0.0	0.00	20.00	0.00	32.89
18	0.0	0.00	16.42	0.00	26.28
19	22.5	0.00	13.36	10.90	15.58
22	0.0	0.00	59.90	50.00	64.60

Lender	4500080000	5000040000	4000060000	5000045000	2000040000
1	36.96	18.88	0.00	0.00	0.00
5	0.00	0.00	0.00	0.00	0.00
8	0.00	0.00	0.00	0.00	0.00
10	0.00	22.95	0.00	0.00	0.00
13	18.97	5.83	15.63	6.67	0.00
16	0.00	0.00	0.00	0.00	0.00
18	0.00	0.00	0.00	0.00	0.00
19	15.63	9.85	0.00	0.00	5.71
22	0.00	57.78	0.00	0.00	0.00

Table A5a: Number of Applications for White Applicants, by Lender and Subset Code

Lender	1000050000	1350080000	1500015000	1500050000	1500050000	1500080000	2000050000	2000050000	2500020000	2500020000	2500025000
1	268	33	0	122	0	127	357	923	0	35	35
3	0	0	0	0	0	0	0	0	0	0	0
4	0	0	0	0	0	0	0	0	0	0	0
5	0	0	0	0	0	0	0	37	0	0	0
6	0	0	0	0	0	0	0	0	0	0	0
7	0	0	0	0	0	0	0	0	0	0	0
8	0	0	0	0	0	0	0	69	0	0	0
9	0	0	0	0	0	0	0	0	0	0	0
10	73	0	0	0	0	0	0	266	0	0	0
11	0	0	0	0	0	0	0	0	0	0	0
12	0	0	0	0	0	0	0	0	0	0	0
13	136	0	0	0	0	35	76	357	0	0	0
14	0	0	0	0	0	0	0	0	0	0	0
15	0	0	0	0	0	0	0	0	0	0	0
16	0	0	0	0	0	0	0	79	0	0	0
17	0	0	0	0	0	0	0	0	0	0	0
18	0	0	0	0	0	0	0	74	0	0	0
19	425	0	0	0	0	51	90	1363	0	0	0
20	0	0	0	0	0	0	0	0	0	0	0
21	0	0	0	0	0	0	0	0	0	0	0
22	48	0	0	0	0	0	45	132	0	0	0

Table A5a: Number of Applications for White Applicants, by Lender and Subset Code (cont'd.)

Lender	2500050000	2500080000	3000050000	3500080000	4000050000	4500080000	5000010000	5000015000
1	67	192	442	129	177	46	283	122
3	0	0	0	0	0	0	0	0
4	0	0	0	0	0	0	0	0
5	0	0	0	0	0	0	0	0
6	0	0	0	0	0	0	0	0
7	0	0	0	0	0	0	0	0
8	0	0	43	0	0	0	0	0
9	0	0	30	0	0	0	0	0
10	0	42	163	0	52	0	60	0
11	0	0	0	0	0	0	0	0
12	0	0	0	0	0	0	0	0
13	0	87	423	113	124	58	125	34
14	0	0	0	0	0	0	0	0
15	0	0	0	0	0	0	0	0
16	0	0	57	0	0	0	0	0
17	0	0	0	0	0	0	0	0
18	0	0	75	0	0	0	0	0
19	49	92	814	68	312	32	420	55
20	0	0	0	0	0	0	0	0
21	0	0	0	0	0	0	0	0
22	0	85	82	33	36	0	41	0

Table A5a: Number of Applications for White Applicants, by Lender and Subset Code (cont'd.)

Lender	5000020000	5000025000	5000030000	5000040000	5000050000	5000060000	5000070000	5000080000
1	1461	55	379	233	90008	706	115	100116
3	0	0	0	0	2448	0	0	2060
4	0	0	0	0	489	0	0	464
5	48	0	0	0	7383	0	0	6479
6	0	0	0	0	159	0	0	152
7	0	0	0	0	1342	0	0	1368
8	108	0	0	0	8211	97	0	10869
9	0	0	0	0	4498	39	35	5097
10	459	0	139	61	41793	299	69	56984
11	0	0	0	0	829	0	0	932
12	0	0	0	0	34	0	0	0
13	550	40	315	120	54815	1499	115	88822
14	0	0	0	0	196	0	0	288
15	0	0	0	0	1554	0	0	1388
16	106	0	40	0	16716	143	0	18239
17	0	0	0	0	903	0	0	736
18	113	0	122	0	16999	214	66	20243
19	2215	55	540	325	168246	1398	96	155503
20	0	0	0	0	2015	35	0	938
21	31	0	0	0	3177	0	0	3004
22	207	0	45	45	13701	598	0	35232

Table A5a: Number of Applications for White Applicants, by Lender and Subset Code (cont'd.)

Lender	6000050000	5000045000	5000051000	5000052000	5100050000	5100051000	5100080000	5200020000
1	422	0	0	0	0	0	0	0
3	0	0	0	0	0	0	0	0
4	0	0	0	0	0	0	0	0
5	0	0	0	0	0	0	0	0
6	0	0	0	0	0	0	0	0
7	0	0	0	0	0	0	0	0
8	0	0	0	0	0	0	0	0
9	0	0	0	0	0	0	0	0
10	170	0	0	0	0	0	0	0
11	0	0	0	0	0	0	0	0
12	0	0	0	0	0	0	0	0
13	509	30	0	0	0	0	0	0
14	0	0	0	0	0	0	0	0
15	0	0	0	0	0	0	0	0
16	61	0	0	0	0	0	0	0
17	0	0	0	0	0	0	0	0
18	46	0	51	39	60	37	95	47
19	668	0	0	0	0	0	0	0
20	0	0	0	0	0	0	0	0
21	0	0	0	0	0	0	0	0
22	181	0	0	0	0	0	0	0

Table A5a: Number of Applications for White Applicants, by Lender and Subset Code (cont'd.)

Lender	5200050000	5200052000	5200080000	5300080000
1	0	0	0	0
3	0	0	0	0
4	0	0	0	0
5	0	0	0	0
6	0	0	0	0
7	0	0	0	0
8	0	0	0	0
9	0	0	0	0
10	0	0	0	0
11	0	0	0	0
12	0	0	0	0
13	0	0	0	0
14	0	0	0	0
15	0	0	0	0
16	0	0	0	0
17	0	0	0	0
18	0	0	0	0
19	47	45	114	62
20	0	0	0	0
21	0	0	0	0
22	0	0	0	0

Table A5b: Percent Denied for White Applicants, by Lender and Subset Code

Lender	1000050000	1350080000	1500015000	1500050000	1500080000	2000050000
1	27.61	33.33	36.89	30.71	40.06	13.76
3	0.00	0.00	0.00	0.00	0.00	0.00
4	0.00	0.00	0.00	0.00	0.00	0.00
5	0.00	0.00	0.00	0.00	0.00	8.11
6	0.00	0.00	0.00	0.00	0.00	0.00
7	0.00	0.00	0.00	0.00	0.00	0.00
8	0.00	0.00	0.00	0.00	0.00	10.14
9	0.00	0.00	0.00	0.00	0.00	0.00
10	9.59	0.00	0.00	0.00	0.00	15.04
11	0.00	0.00	0.00	0.00	0.00	0.00
12	0.00	0.00	0.00	0.00	0.00	0.00
13	13.97	0.00	0.00	17.14	11.84	6.72
14	0.00	0.00	0.00	0.00	0.00	0.00
15	0.00	0.00	0.00	0.00	0.00	0.00
16	0.00	0.00	0.00	0.00	0.00	5.06
17	0.00	0.00	0.00	0.00	0.00	0.00
18	0.00	0.00	0.00	0.00	0.00	8.11
19	13.18	0.00	0.00	13.73	12.22	6.31
20	0.00	0.00	0.00	0.00	0.00	0.00
21	0.00	0.00	0.00	0.00	0.00	0.00
22	68.75	0.00	0.00	0.00	66.67	59.09

Table A5b: Percent Denied for White Applicants, by Lender and Subset Code (cont'd.)

Lender	2500020000	2500025000	2500050000	2500080000	3000050000	3500080000
1	17.14	22.86	25.37	23.96	29.86	36.43
3	0.00	0.00	0.00	0.00	0.00	0.00
4	0.00	0.00	0.00	0.00	0.00	0.00
5	0.00	0.00	0.00	0.00	0.00	0.00
6	0.00	0.00	0.00	0.00	0.00	0.00
7	0.00	0.00	0.00	0.00	0.00	0.00
8	0.00	0.00	0.00	0.00	9.30	0.00
9	0.00	0.00	0.00	0.00	26.67	0.00
10	0.00	0.00	0.00	16.67	17.79	0.00
11	0.00	0.00	0.00	0.00	0.00	0.00
12	0.00	0.00	0.00	0.00	0.00	0.00
13	0.00	0.00	0.00	10.34	11.82	14.16
14	0.00	0.00	0.00	0.00	0.00	0.00
15	0.00	0.00	0.00	0.00	0.00	0.00
16	0.00	0.00	0.00	0.00	33.33	0.00
17	0.00	0.00	0.00	0.00	0.00	0.00
18	0.00	0.00	0.00	0.00	5.33	0.00
19	0.00	0.00	6.12	15.22	12.78	30.88
20	0.00	0.00	0.00	0.00	0.00	0.00
21	0.00	0.00	0.00	0.00	0.00	0.00
22	0.00	0.00	0.00	67.06	54.88	69.70

Table A5b: Percent Denied for White Applicants, by Lender and Subset Code (cont'd.)

Lender	4000050000	4500080000	5000010000	5000015000	5000020000	5000025000
1	15.25	36.96	26.15	30.33	11.91	25.45
3	0.00	0.00	0.00	0.00	0.00	0.00
4	0.00	0.00	0.00	0.00	0.00	0.00
5	0.00	0.00	0.00	0.00	4.17	0.00
6	0.00	0.00	0.00	0.00	0.00	0.00
7	0.00	0.00	0.00	0.00	0.00	0.00
8	0.00	0.00	0.00	0.00	3.70	0.00
9	0.00	0.00	0.00	0.00	0.00	0.00
10	19.23	0.00	18.33	0.00	13.29	0.00
11	0.00	0.00	0.00	0.00	0.00	0.00
12	0.00	0.00	0.00	0.00	0.00	0.00
13	13.71	18.97	12.80	20.59	8.91	7.50
14	0.00	0.00	0.00	0.00	0.00	0.00
15	0.00	0.00	0.00	0.00	0.00	0.00
16	0.00	0.00	0.00	0.00	10.38	0.00
17	0.00	0.00	0.00	0.00	0.00	0.00
18	0.00	0.00	0.00	0.00	6.19	0.00
19	10.90	15.63	13.33	14.55	5.10	20.00
20	0.00	0.00	0.00	0.00	0.00	0.00
21	0.00	0.00	0.00	0.00	9.68	0.00
22	50.00	0.00	56.10	0.00	56.04	0.00

Table A5b: Percent Denied for White Applicants, by Lender and Subset Code (cont'd.)

Lender	5000030000	5000040000	5000050000	5000060000	5000070000	5000080000
1	27.70	18.88	16.67	17.14	1.74	22.46
3	0.00	0.00	2.33	0.00	0.00	4.13
4	0.00	0.00	15.54	0.00	0.00	13.36
5	0.00	0.00	4.37	0.00	0.00	9.92
6	0.00	0.00	13.21	0.00	0.00	33.55
7	0.00	0.00	4.40	0.00	0.00	8.04
8	0.00	0.00	3.74	6.19	0.00	6.01
9	0.00	0.00	6.11	2.56	0.00	11.36
10	17.99	22.95	12.35	17.06	14.49	14.56
11	0.00	0.00	17.97	0.00	0.00	24.46
12	0.00	0.00	2.94	0.00	0.00	0.00
13	13.02	5.83	9.07	14.61	14.78	13.44
14	0.00	0.00	28.57	0.00	0.00	19.10
15	0.00	0.00	10.81	0.00	0.00	14.84
16	35.00	0.00	12.50	41.96	0.00	22.19
17	0.00	0.00	9.41	0.00	0.00	11.82
18	5.74	0.00	7.92	8.41	0.00	11.74
19	13.15	9.85	6.68	10.16	11.46	11.01
20	0.00	0.00	7.64	14.29	0.00	11.09
21	0.00	0.00	7.33	0.00	0.00	7.66
22	57.78	57.78	56.86	63.21	0.00	62.63

Table A5b: Percent Denied for White Applicants, by Lender and Subset Code (cont'd.)

Lender	6000050000	5000045000	5000051000	5000052000	5100050000	5100051000
1	17.30	0.00	0.00	0.00	0.00	0.00
3	0.00	0.00	0.00	0.00	0.00	0.00
4	0.00	0.00	0.00	0.00	0.00	0.00
5	0.00	0.00	0.00	0.00	0.00	0.00
6	0.00	0.00	0.00	0.00	0.00	0.00
7	0.00	0.00	0.00	0.00	0.00	0.00
8	0.00	0.00	0.00	0.00	0.00	0.00
9	0.00	0.00	0.00	0.00	0.00	0.00
10	13.53	0.00	0.00	0.00	0.00	0.00
11	0.00	0.00	0.00	0.00	0.00	0.00
12	0.00	0.00	0.00	0.00	0.00	0.00
13	14.73	6.67	0.00	0.00	0.00	0.00
14	0.00	0.00	0.00	0.00	0.00	0.00
15	0.00	0.00	0.00	0.00	0.00	0.00
16	24.59	0.00	0.00	0.00	0.00	0.00
17	0.00	0.00	0.00	0.00	0.00	0.00
18	6.52	0.00	0.00	0.00	0.00	0.00
19	11.23	0.00	21.57	10.26	21.67	10.81
20	0.00	0.00	0.00	0.00	0.00	0.00
21	0.00	0.00	0.00	0.00	0.00	0.00
22	65.19	0.00	0.00	0.00	0.00	0.00

Table A5b: Percent Denied for White Applicants, by Lender and Subset Code (cont'd.)

Lender	5100080000	5200020000	5200050000	5200052000	5200080000	5300080000
1	0	0.00	0.00	0.00	0.00	0.00
3	0	0.00	0.00	0.00	0.00	0.00
4	0	0.00	0.00	0.00	0.00	0.00
5	0	0.00	0.00	0.00	0.00	0.00
6	0	0.00	0.00	0.00	0.00	0.00
7	0	0.00	0.00	0.00	0.00	0.00
8	0	0.00	0.00	0.00	0.00	0.00
9	0	0.00	0.00	0.00	0.00	0.00
10	0	0.00	0.00	0.00	0.00	0.00
11	0	0.00	0.00	0.00	0.00	0.00
12	0	0.00	0.00	0.00	0.00	0.00
13	0	0.00	0.00	0.00	0.00	0.00
14	0	0.00	0.00	0.00	0.00	0.00
15	0	0.00	0.00	0.00	0.00	0.00
16	0	0.00	0.00	0.00	0.00	0.00
17	0	0.00	0.00	0.00	0.00	0.00
18	0	0.00	0.00	0.00	0.00	0.00
19	20	6.38	10.64	4.44	9.65	27.42
20	0	0.00	0.00	0.00	0.00	0.00
21	0	0.00	0.00	0.00	0.00	0.00
22	0	0.00	0.00	0.00	0.00	0.00

Table A6a: Number of Applications for Hispanics, by Lender and Subset Code

Lender	11	12	13	15	21	14	31
1	15111	2483	81	26546	2723	0	0
3	62	34	0	127	56	0	0
4	294	0	0	259	0	0	0
5	264	61	0	433	51	0	0
7	116	0	0	230	36	0	0
8	557	118	0	1322	146	0	0
9	92	69	0	226	74	0	0
10	4300	680	39	13393	756	0	0
11	33	0	0	65	0	58	0
13	6897	1296	389	20385	1315	0	152
14	0	0	0	43	0	0	0
15	55	0	0	83	0	0	0
16	519	184	0	1286	191	0	0
17	38	0	0	44	0	0	0
18	1173	220	160	2558	326	0	0
19	9466	3932	0	18466	4178	0	70
20	82	0	0	128	0	0	0
21	246	42	0	282	68	0	0
22	2768	346	105	10601	379	0	37

Table A6b: Percent Denied for Hispanics, by Lender and Subset Code

Lender	11	12	13	15	21	14	31
1	38.3694	22.3520	22.2222	39.4146	21.3000	0.0000	0.0000
3	16.1290	2.9412	0.0000	7.8740	3.5714	0.0000	0.0000
4	25.1701	0.0000	0.0000	20.4633	0.0000	0.0000	0.0000
5	15.9091	6.5574	0.0000	21.9400	1.9608	0.0000	0.0000
7	16.3793	0.0000	0.0000	23.0435	11.1111	0.0000	0.0000
8	8.4381	5.9322	0.0000	10.1362	7.5342	0.0000	0.0000
9	13.0435	13.0435	0.0000	19.4690	10.8108	0.0000	0.0000
10	18.9302	13.5294	30.7692	18.8233	13.3598	6.8966	0.0000
11	42.4242	0.0000	0.0000	27.6923	0.0000	0.0000	0.0000
13	15.8475	9.4907	14.9100	18.4891	10.2662	0.0000	13.8158
14	0.0000	0.0000	0.0000	32.5581	0.0000	0.0000	0.0000
15	30.9091	0.0000	0.0000	19.2771	0.0000	0.0000	0.0000
16	36.9942	20.6522	0.0000	43.2348	21.4660	0.0000	0.0000
17	23.6842	0.0000	0.0000	20.4545	0.0000	0.0000	0.0000
18	18.4996	12.7273	0.0000	19.5856	11.9632	0.0000	0.0000
19	17.0188	9.2065	20.0000	20.5188	9.3107	0.0000	15.7143
20	17.0732	0.0000	0.0000	4.6875	0.0000	0.0000	0.0000
21	9.3496	7.1429	0.0000	7.4468	7.3529	0.0000	0.0000
22	59.6821	57.2254	60.9524	67.5314	60.1583	0.0000	59.4595

Table A7a: Number of Applications for Non-Hispanics, by Lender and Subset Code

Lender	12	21	22	23	25	32
1	2483	2723	93238	688	108153	232
3	34	56	2405	0	2221	0
4	0	0	280	0	379	0
5	61	51	7824	0	7337	0
6	0	0	167	0	178	0
7	0	36	1289	0	1347	0
8	118	146	9655	119	13890	0
9	69	74	4492	0	5543	0
10	680	756	42877	392	57574	164
11	0	0	873	0	1134	0
13	1296	1315	56696	1354	96213	325
14	0	0	209	0	399	0
15	0	0	1542	0	1386	0
16	184	191	17215	143	19752	49
17	0	0	1028	0	821	0
18	220	326	17550	169	22485	82
19	3932	4178	176792	1639	171753	761
20	0	0	1890	0	845	0
21	42	68	3351	0	3316	0
22	346	379	14339	597	36698	159

Table A7b: Percent Denied for Non-Hispanics, by Lender and Subset Code

Lender	12	21	22	23	25	32
1	22.3520	21.3000	15.1494	16.4244	21.3383	18.9655
3	2.9412	3.5714	2.1206	0.0000	5.2229	0.0000
4	0.0000	0.0000	2.1429	0.0000	5.8047	0.0000
5	6.5574	1.9608	4.2434	0.0000	11.0536	0.0000
6	0.0000	0.0000	16.1677	0.0000	38.7640	0.0000
7	0.0000	11.1111	3.4911	0.0000	6.6073	0.0000
8	5.9322	7.5342	3.9772	5.0420	6.4435	0.0000
9	13.0435	10.8108	6.3001	0.0000	12.0332	0.0000
10	13.5294	13.3598	12.5825	14.5408	14.8313	13.4146
11	0.0000	0.0000	17.9840	0.0000	26.2787	0.0000
13	9.4907	10.2662	9.2987	15.6573	13.9565	15.0769
14	0.0000	0.0000	29.6651	0.0000	19.7995	0.0000
15	0.0000	0.0000	9.8573	0.0000	14.8629	0.0000
16	20.6522	21.4660	12.4891	41.9580	23.2382	24.4898
17	0.0000	0.0000	9.2412	0.0000	11.9367	0.0000
18	12.7273	11.9632	8.2507	5.9172	12.8263	8.5366
19	9.2065	9.3107	6.5948	10.1891	11.3180	9.4612
20	0.0000	0.0000	7.9365	0.0000	12.4260	0.0000
21	7.1429	7.3529	7.2814	0.0000	8.0217	0.0000
22	57.2254	60.1583	55.7640	62.6466	59.3275	67.9245

Table A8a: Number of Applications for Female Applicants, by Lender and Subset Code

Lender	12	21	22	23	24	25	32
1	85901	22732	3225	163	45	55728	145
3	2399	203	45	0	0	1070	0
4	497	116	0	0	0	308	0
5	7164	976	153	0	0	3578	0
6	145	0	0	0	0	72	0
7	1304	140	46	0	0	774	0
8	8829	1574	295	0	0	6904	0
9	4401	602	90	0	0	2576	0
10	43864	7011	1244	54	77	32254	159
11	808	117	0	0	0	572	0
12	38	0	0	0	0	0	0
13	57233	11884	1938	398	79	53677	172
14	185	52	0	0	0	255	0
15	1233	352	38	0	0	678	0
16	15672	2260	306	35	0	9067	41
17	1036	136	0	0	0	382	0
18	16454	3337	466	36	0	11180	0
19	168121	28396	4474	202	57	82370	194
20	2038	107	0	0	0	350	0
21	3016	477	86	0	0	1564	0
22	16847	2399	383	115	0	20956	64

Table A8b: Percent Denied for Female Applicants, by Lender and Subset Code

Lender	12	21	22	23	24	25	32
1	16.7809	20.5349	28.8682	17.7914	2.2222	23.5519	28.2759
3	2.2926	4.9261	6.6667	0.0000	0.0000	4.2991	0.0000
4	13.6821	10.3448	0.0000	0.0000	0.0000	12.0130	0.0000
5	4.2434	5.8402	8.4967	0.0000	0.0000	10.5646	0.0000
6	14.4828	0.0000	0.0000	0.0000	0.0000	40.2778	0.0000
7	3.8344	7.8571	8.6957	0.0000	0.0000	8.0103	0.0000
8	3.9529	5.7179	7.4576	0.0000	0.0000	6.9670	0.0000
9	5.7941	8.9701	7.7778	0.0000	0.0000	11.9565	0.0000
10	12.5160	15.9036	17.3633	9.2593	9.0909	15.3128	12.5786
11	17.2030	26.4957	0.0000	0.0000	0.0000	26.0490	0.0000
12	7.8947	0.0000	0.0000	0.0000	0.0000	0.0000	0.0000
13	9.4596	12.6304	14.1899	22.6131	21.5190	14.7549	16.2791
14	29.7297	26.9231	0.0000	0.0000	0.0000	19.2157	0.0000
15	10.0568	12.5000	13.1579	0.0000	0.0000	13.4218	0.0000
16	12.6787	20.8850	22.8758	42.8571	0.0000	23.9771	19.5122
17	9.6525	11.0294	0.0000	0.0000	0.0000	9.9476	0.0000
18	7.8400	10.3386	13.5193	5.5556	0.0000	12.1020	0.0000
19	6.6488	10.2233	10.1475	28.2178	10.5263	12.2265	15.4639
20	7.3602	14.9533	0.0000	0.0000	0.0000	11.1429	0.0000
21	7.2944	8.1761	8.1395	0.0000	0.0000	7.5448	0.0000
22	56.4789	60.9004	63.9687	52.1739	0.0000	61.2187	67.1875

Table A9a: Number of Applications for Male Applicants, by Lender and Subset Code

Lender	11	12	13	14	15	21	31
1	4101	85901	362	113	80640	22732	68
3	52	2399	0	0	1426	203	0
4	0	497	0	0	380	116	0
5	161	7164	0	0	4351	976	0
6	0	145	0	0	114	0	0
7	52	1304	0	0	858	140	0
8	270	8829	82	0	8867	1574	0
9	71	4401	0	0	3473	602	0
10	1435	43864	185	94	43913	7011	72
11	0	808	0	0	659	117	0
12	0	38	0	0	0	0	0
13	2093	57233	996	112	73969	11884	59
14	0	185	0	0	225	52	0
15	0	1233	0	0	815	352	0
16	561	15672	90	0	12643	2260	0
17	50	1036	0	0	584	136	0
18	626	16454	84	74	15360	3337	0
19	5430	168121	556	77	118435	28396	59
20	32	2038	0	0	692	107	0
21	133	3016	0	0	2040	477	0
22	593	16847	399	0	30813	2399	0

Table A9b: Percent Denied for Male Applicants, by Lender and Subset Code

Lender	11	12	13	14	15	21	31
1	31.1144	16.7809	18.5083	2.6549	25.6634	20.5349	16.1765
3	0.0000	2.2926	0.0000	0.0000	6.1010	4.9261	0.0000
4	0.0000	13.6821	0.0000	0.0000	10.5263	10.3448	0.0000
5	8.6957	4.2434	0.0000	0.0000	12.3880	5.8402	0.0000
6	0.0000	14.4828	0.0000	0.0000	38.5965	0.0000	0.0000
7	9.6154	3.8344	0.0000	0.0000	9.4406	7.8571	0.0000
8	7.7778	3.9529	10.9756	0.0000	6.7554	5.7179	0.0000
9	12.6761	5.7941	0.0000	0.0000	12.2661	8.9701	0.0000
10	14.5645	12.5160	20.0000	12.7660	15.8791	15.9036	19.4444
11	0.0000	17.2030	0.0000	0.0000	26.2519	26.4957	0.0000
12	0.0000	7.8947	0.0000	0.0000	0.0000	0.0000	0.0000
13	14.2379	9.4596	15.6627	16.0714	15.2023	12.6304	18.6441
14	0.0000	29.7297	0.0000	0.0000	23.1111	26.9231	0.0000
15	0.0000	10.0568	0.0000	0.0000	16.8098	12.5000	0.0000
16	19.1136	12.6787	42.2222	0.0000	26.2517	20.8850	0.0000
17	26.0000	9.6525	0.0000	0.0000	14.7260	11.0294	0.0000
18	17.2524	7.8400	3.5714	0.0000	13.9779	10.3386	0.0000
19	10.0184	6.6488	15.2878	7.7922	12.4279	10.2233	13.5593
20	18.7500	7.3602	0.0000	0.0000	11.2717	14.9533	0.0000
21	6.7669	7.2944	0.0000	0.0000	8.3824	8.1761	0.0000
22	68.9713	56.4789	61.6541	0.0000	62.1751	60.9004	0.0000